# Styx

I0103272

## *Khaos*

**chipmunkapublishing**

the mental health publisher

Published by

Chipmunkapublishing

PO Box 6872

Brentwood

Essex CM13 1ZT

United Kingdom

**http://www.chipmunkapublishing.com**

Edited by Aleks Lech

Chipmunkapublishing gratefully acknowledge the support of Arts Council England.

## Author Biography

Categorized as psychotic over ten years ago, Khaos has undergone the shame and stigmatization of being referred to as mentally ill. The diagnoses used to describe this condition have included schizophrenia, paranoid-delusional, bi-polar, and depressed. The author has refused the categories and pursued a Ph.D. in Anthropology at Stanford University. Khaos graduated from Harvard University with an A.B. in History and Literature and the University of Chicago with a masters in Social Science. She has recently been accepted to medical school. Born in Evanston, Illinois in 1972 and writing all her life, the author has never before attempted to document what is considered so taboo in her family and society at large: psychosis. To contact the author, please write to khaos_2010@yahoo.com

Khaos

**Styx I**

"Sticks and stones may break my bones but words can never hurt me..."

Childhood rhyme.

"This river Styx served as a crossroads where the world of the living met the world of the dead, and the world of the mortal met the world of the immortal.   Greek Mythology Gods, mortals, and great heroes and villains made their way across the river Styx. Some crossed the river many times, but for most, it was a one way trip."

http://www.theriverstyx.net/

"Lay 'em down, Sethe. Sword and shield.  Down. Down. Both of 'em down.  Down by the riverside.  Sword and shield.  Don't study war no more.  Lay all that mess down.  Sword and shield."

Baby Suggs to Sethe in Toni Morrison's *Beloved*

Timeline

1994 - First trip to India

1997 - Second trip to India

1999 - Third trip to India

1999 - First hospitalisation

2001-2003 - Trip to Tibet

September-December 2003 - Return to Evanston

May 2004 - Dalai Lama visits U.S. I

November 2005 - Dalai Lama visits U.S. II

April 2006 - Dalai Lama visits U.S. III

December 2006 - Return to Evanston

June 2007 - Second hospitalisation

November 2007 - January 2008 - Third hospitalisation

## Chapter 1

This book is a future book. Not a present book. I am not ready to write this book. Just to pre-shade it.

Psychotic.

There it is.

The word.

The hate.

The, dare I say it?, name.

What disease?

Psychosis.

That's what. And so I keep on writing to let you, the reader, know what it means to be sick, when you're not really sick. Or so they tell you. Or so you tell yourself. Because 94 pounds is not sick. I still don't believe it is sick, which is why I am not ready to write this book.

Peeing in a cup. Masticating cabbage. "Biling." Because I knew the body could regenerate itself.

If I just lie still the medicine will excrete

ooze

expunge

out of the body.

Outside. Every last drop, fraction, bit.

I can see my bones.

Bones are beautiful.

Jutting out as they do.

Christ.  They don't believe me.

I am a doctor (a PhD.).

Do I stutter?

I take the Lord's name in vain.

Because, Christ, nobody believes me.

And so I testify

(...write this book).

Sleep.  It calls to me.  Adieu for now.

Next day.  I still have so many fragments of me.

That  I am trying to piece

together

like so many wedges on a hand sewn quilt.

Skin as fabric

Blood as annealing matter...

Drops of medicine seep out of me.

Eliminate-ing

Evacuate-ing

Purge-ing

the medicine.

That is my major concern.

## Styx

I must rid the body of all traces

for it is poison.

Unnatural.

Unholy.

Separate from me.

Their pleas fall on deaf ears.

I do not listen.

For their words are poison like the medicine.

They are one and the same.

Terrors infiltrating the veins.

Heart.

Blood.

Away! AWAY!!

And so I lay in the room. Quiet so no one could hear me.

A breath.

A being.

I must separate out like alcohol distilled from water.

No convergence.

Convergence is verboten.

Like the holocaust to a Jew.

Away!  AWAY!!

The body cannot stand the contamination of food, water, touch, feel, sensation, beings.

Purity stands in isolation.

The light stays on through the night.

Until I suspect someone suspects the body's presence.

And then I turn it off.

All goes dark.

I am alone at last under the blankets.

A final resting place.

A sanctuary.

Away from the noise.

The people.

The pollution.

I bought the fuchsia, mealy, stuffed blanket-comforter with a satin and cotton side with the mom's money.

Like I paid the rent in that god-forsaken wooden apartment with the mom's money.

Like I paid for tuition at Harvard Extension school.

It is all of a circle.  One work.

Just dirty.  That's all.

And so I escaped,

bills paid in full,

into my cocoon.

Dry-heat-ridden nest of a room.

My window faced out onto the wooden exterior of the building next door.

Periodically, shocks sparked from the transformer attached to the pole climbing the exterior of the bildenplatz.

I swear I could feel them riveting the body - one electric shock after the next - every time I saw sparks fly. I imagined myself the patient of shock-therapy. A last cruel vestige of madhouses of the past.

I cried out in pain,

muffled the head into the pillow, and waited to hear the reverberation of my voice through the garbage alley between our two bildungen: glass and bottle rocks picking up the sound and passing it through an index of refraction beyond my comprehension. But somebody knew what it meant.

And so I waited.

For Godot.

Alone, however.

To my wanting.

It scares me to write this way. Alienating me from the people around me.

Christ.

There it is again.

Taking the Lord's name in vain.

God forgive me.

I waited for the medicine to expunge from the body.

Like wine from the hands and feet of Jesus on the cross.

An elixir for some.

A poison to the body.

The purifying substance is the poison.

The poison is the purifying substance.

Nothing is clean again.

## Chapter 2

Some things cannot be written.  Like the pain in the mother's voice aching after me for fear that I was dying.

I knew in my bones she was crazy.

And that was why she was calling me crazy.

Psychotic.

There it is again.

The word.

The name.

And my brother in cahoots.

The doctors.

All allied against me.

Unified.

In their effort to cure me.

I was not sick.

I am not sick.

But they keep looking out for the body.  Just to make sure.  You never know.

The brain was just too much.

So it had to be named to be tamed.

Psychotic.

Ellipse.

Or was it eclipse?

The Boston/Somerville/Cambridge era of my post-post-graduate days. Seven months in limbo that all began with a power struggle back in Evanston between mother and daughter over who would control the oars of the boat.

Sticks and stones may break my bones...

After all, I was a doctor (a PhD.) now.

But the rest is not history. Oh no! Hell no! The rest is the future.

Unknown, treacherous, thorny path.

## Chapter 3

Sleeping beauty waited.

And waited.

And much to her chagrin.  They showed up.

Fire station and all.  With dispatcher and Dr. brother.  To collect their bounty.  Prize.

Wrest it from the rightful owners.  The maternally hip landlord to whom the mother's rent checks went each month.

She too professed concern and so was not altogether safe.

## Chapter 4

Even the cabbage was the body's enemy.

Silence was my only friend.

Who never came.

Just shades of silence.

Echoing voices down the hall. Reverberations of the room mate's stereo. Sounds of sex penetrating the ceiling below. The wooden floor could not hold all those secrets.

The cocoon. The nest disintegrated with each sound.

## Chapter 5

Telephone messages accumulated.

"Mom called. She is in town. She is worried about you."

"Mom called. Brother is on his way."

Family (There it is. The name.) kept encroaching.

"Mom called. Return call."

Until finally, the room mate let the brother (and his wife) inside.

Needle-thorns slaughtered.

Protective shielding gone.

With the dispatcher on the line, the entire (or so it seemed) Cambridge fire force (backed up by police force) called itself in at the brother's plea for help. His sword not big enough? Ha!

I blockaded the door.

He pushed me back. Laughing.

They arrived. I greeted each and every one with a shake of the hand. Thanked them and bid them farewell.

They would not listen to me. Only Dr. brother.

## Chapter 6

It was the third time the medical family had called in reinforcements on me. It was not to be the last.

## Chapter 7

And so they picked the body up by the shirtsleeves that covered it. Placed it in a chair. And strapped it in.

I smiled. I thanked them in whispers.

I hated.

The brother's wife poked around the apartment. What was she looking for?

"I trust you!"

I knew she would not steal anything. (Being adopted and Korean.)

((Which meant everything of course.))

The final wrist restraints (snap! snap!) in place, sleeping beauty was removed from the den. Neighbours a-gawk, room mate watching television.

## Chapter 8

And so now I look back on this event (these events - there were so many) and know.

Crime occurs.

Criminals get away with murder.

Love sanctifies all actions.

Even death.

Jews remember the holocaust.

Even when it sprang from a place of love.

## Chapter 9

I remember the ambulance ride to the hospital. The fire officers remained by my side the entire time/way. I stared out the back window. It reminded me of another ambulance ride. But that is a story for another time and place. This ambulance ride brought me to the steps of the psychiatric emergency entrance (I did not know they had a separate entrance at the time) where they (I am not ready to write this), the driver and the two fire officers, dropped me. Like a child going to school for the first time. The chair rolled. I looked up before the doors closed in on me.

"I got blue!"

A direct reference to the colour of the sky on a clear autumn evening. Was it summer still? I did not feel a chill.

Dr. brother kept talking and wife by his side helping. He directed the action that directed us.

I began telling time for the workers, knowing full-well they hated what they were doing and were dying to get off. They removed the plastic wrist restraints and replaced them with a numbered tag: Jennifer Marie Chertow D.O.B.: 05/29/72 There was no doubting that identity. It was there in black ink. I ripped off the bracelet. Dr. brother kept talking. They must have driven there.

Directing the action that directed us, Dr. brother gave them instructions; "she needs an I.V.", and so they rolled me into "the first available room," injected a needle into my arm, and flew in fluid. The nurse, bright-eyed, blonde, young, looked at me, smiled, fixed the bag hanging from a stand. The liquid flowed into my arm through the needle. Machines beeped behind me, and an officer affixed his gaze on me. "I'd shoot her!" he said. Another, black officer, joined him, tried to distract him, laughed with him. The body rejected the bag. Blood swept into the bag. I lifted the red tube to show the first officer. "This is good!?"

I questioned the entire operation.

And so the blonde nurse got another bag. Got another needle. Dr. brother interjecting all the time, wife flitting around beside him, "The bag was rejected!" I was proud of my body. *Keep going*, I urged it, *you're doing good!* And so it rejected the second bag as well. This time the officer came by to inspect. As if I could reject the bag by (obvious) will or had meddled with the tubing.

I can't tell you anymore right now.

## Chapter 10

My birthday was just yesterday! We went to the Drake; it had been a year since the second hospitalisation and return home. The third had followed, but there I was. I was so proud! Mom, sister, and I sat at the table and drank tea out of white porcelain. It seemed right. Itty-bitty sandwiches, a harp, a skinny, cutting-edge, Indian host. All the pieces (seemed to) fell in place. I was happy. Genuinely happy. I could take advantage of my mother once again. No, no, no, Jen. You're not taking advantage of your mother. She loves you.

Somebody was saying that to me, anyway.

People say that.

I know the truth. I got lots of presents that birthday. $1000.00, jewellery, gauzy shirts, but best of all I got tea at the Drake and public acknowledgement of my birthday. Guilt money. Guilt gifts. And public accolades of me. Cousin Jack committed suicide, but that wasn't until later. Yesterday to be precise. Whew! Glad I got that off my chest. And so the gifts and cards kept pouring in. It wasn't all that much, actually. But it felt like a million bucks after what they'd put me through. I deserved it. I'd earned it. I'd paid my debt to society and now it was payback time.

Hate.

It drives a girl insane.

Love.

It sustains.

I see the future as I see myself.

A broken reflection. A disturbed pond surface.

Mirroring back an ugly/beautiful image that I only half recognize.

The swift wind ruffles the edge of my gauzy shirt - disturbs the surface of the pond.

Love.

Life is an endless quest for (unrequited?) love. In family relationships. Love relationships. Friendships. And I seek love in my darkest relationships. Patient/doctor. A resolution to pain inflicted. Guilt (theirs - not mine) resolved. Can time really heal? Can we really forgive the (personal/-systemic) violence? When we draw lines, what lines get erased?

# Chapter 11

I am not ready to write this book.

## Chapter 12

The body revolts in pain.  Do not touch me!  I cannot scream.

"Liz, you have to look!"

I force my sister.

She screams back,

"I love you, Jen!"

Or did she say "we"?

Is she complicit? (I know. She is.)

In the abuse.

Hand on privates.  (Not my hand.)

Trying to...

"Liz, you have to look!"

My voice plays again in my head.  I say nothing because by this time the offending officer has stopped masturbating (there it is, the name) me.  Strapped into a body board as if I had fallen.  Broken my back.

"I can't breathe!" I go back, for you, the reader, to my second complaint to them (the first being the third), the fire officers/police enforcers.

"I've called people, Jen!"  The mother screams across the kitchen table at me as I run, frantic, around the house, wearing a purple "Move!" tee-shirt over a white, long sleeved tee, trying to escape, to hide.  Like a child.

People.

What was I?

"I don't know you! I don't know you! I don't know you!" A desperate mantra repeated a hundred times in the face of power. So deep was my faith in Foucault, I was convinced it would work. This was my original communication to the fire officers/police enforcers.

"She knows not to recognize."

A chink in their chain.

I broke free of their enclosing circle and made a run for the parents' room. Seeking safety. Sanctuary.

They would not dare enter.

I blockaded the door.

Two men and a woman pushed their way in. I had no defenses left. Breathless, struggling for breath, I gave up.

They wrestled me downstairs and out of the front door like a stranger.

I called out to my imprisoners, complicit sisters, "If I go to the hospital, you have to come with me and stay there." My meaning: If I'm sick, so are you.

"I flew in to bring you to the hospital, Jen" the older sister informed me not an hour before. A warning.

I pretended to watch T.V.

What crime? They would find - for I knew in the end it would result in the scene that played out - me watching T.V. It's what people did every day. Some all day, every day. I was just watching T.V.

I am not sick.

Another ambulance ride. The second of three. The third of which you have already heard.

I focused on the pavement I could see passing beneath out of the back window. Not unlike the first ambulance ride. Another story for another time.

Like some sick parody, she had to touch my privates.

I'll never be able to fathom why.

Did she envision controlling me somehow? A prison playmate?

"That's sexual harassment!" I cried when I saw that the sister saw. What I meant was assault. But what could I do strapped to a board? My vocabulary was limited, and I already knew I had to be careful.

Yes, there was the threat of being thrown in jail.

For what crime, I'll never be able to fathom, but I knew the accuser was the mother.

Interloper!

Milker!

Was I milking my mother for all she was worth? I did not even have a chance to spring to my own defense when I heard one of the men wrapping me up say, "I think this could be a case of invasion of privacy." At first, I thought he was coming to my defense, but then it dawned on me that I was being cast in the role of criminal. I am infringing on my parents' privacy. I still, a part of me still, hopes I am wrong.

I'll never know.

Does it matter?

I know where I ended up.

At the local-commercial-private-community-health-centre.

That is, home for the (criminally?) insane.

En route, they dosed me up at the hospital with a sedative in front of an entire police squadron waiting to pounce on the psychotic. For certainly that must have been the term the mother used to describe the "situation."

I believe there was compassion in their voice. Their collective fire officer/police enforcer voice.

The touch...? Misplaced compassion?

Germans loved the Jews, too.

At the end of the day, I'll never know.

## Chapter 13

Fight!  If you can, fight!

I fought and did not have to take the medicine that time.

I ended up barefoot, walking home by the lake to retrieve my driver's license and ATM cards.

I was outta there.

Boston, here I come!

And so that was how I ended up enrolled at Harvard Extension that fall and sleeping away the summer before in Somerville.

It  was not long before medicine caught up with me.  In hounding telephone messages.

"Mom called.  Call back."

And I ended up in the hospital for the third and final (?) time.

Mother and Dr. brother were at it again.  As you, the reader, already know.

## Chapter 14

This is my future book.  I am not sick, and yet they still force me to voluntarily take medicine and see a psychiatrist.

I no longer try to purge the medicine from my system.  But I know it taints me.

No matter how much I try to convince myself that it purifies me, or at the very least is indifferent to me.

I try not to care, too.

For every line I try to erase another line is drawn.  My life is replete with boxes.  My past, a PhD.  My future, an M.D.  Where do I fit in?  How do I accommodate all the contradictions?  Confluences?  It is a myriad rivers converging into oceans and diverging into rivulets.

My greatest fear?  Nothing holds water.  It is all hot air.  A puff of smoke.  Smoke and mirrors.  The centre does not hold.  Things fall apart.

In which country do we reside?  Which continent?  Africa?  Colonized Africa?

## Chapter 15

The pavement rushed beneath the ambulance as in the first ambulance ride.

## Chapter 16

The pavement rushed beneath the ambulance as I watched the scene pass outside the back window. A Sikh doctor, Indian intern, and Oxford English medical student attended to me in the ambulance. They were taking me from Dharamsala to Delhi. I had made it the other way all by myself. On pre-dissertation research. Researching torture victims, human rights claims, refugees. I got stuck on the Dalai Lama. I thought I could set up a meeting with him as a graduate researcher. I was wrong. My efforts got me into hot water, and my parents were contacted by the U.S. embassy to bring me home. Hence, the ambulance ride. I did have a "meeting" with the Dalai Lama before I was sent back to the U.S. He hugged me and said "take care." I got no information for the research.

The rest is not history. It is the future.

I was put on medicine, returned to the U.S. (Dr. brother flew to India to pick me up), and hospitalised for nine days. They kept me on the medicine for the next nine months. I convinced a doctor at Stanford to taper me off the medicine. I remained off of it for the next three years. During this time, I lived in Tibet. When I returned to the U.S., I called the psychiatrist initially in charge of my care upon return from India. I told him I was scared and had just passed out. Truths. He put me on the medicine again. I remained on it for the next four years until, eventually, I started lactating from the side effects.

This time, I tapered myself off of the medicine under the supervision of two separate psychiatrists. It resulted in two separate hospitalisations. As you, the reader, know. All at the behest of my mother. The doctor.

Love?

Hate?

Are the two so different?

Two sides of the same coin.

## Chapter 17

Relations between first and third world are not so clear cut. Individuals get caught between the cracks. As a researcher, I never cast myself into the role of individual. But the die is cast. What is a dividual? An in-dividual? Somehow we are not divided? Composed of many parts? That is the lie. Writing, I am trying to reveal the lie.

And power.

And money.

And fame.

And vaingloriousness.

Structures structure us into place. Determine our existence. Pre-conditions for all events. We are not free. But to lose the quest for freedom is death.

## Chapter 18

I took off my heavy boots, hiking boots. Bill went in front of me. The water rushed around our feet. Stones pressed into our toes. Early fall waters, icy, numbed our feet. With the heavy pack on the back, I did not think I would make it. We forded. The waters gave way. We crossed, safely, to the other side. The sun came out. Brightened our way. I smiled.

The Khali Gandaki had withered away to a rivulet in areas, but here we forded a rushing stream.

*Momos* and apple pies awaited us on the other side. How hospitable were the Nepalese people we encountered on that Annapurna trip. I was just out of college. The world my oyster.

# Chapter 19

It pains me to write this.

I love my family.

I love my mother.

I love my sisters,

my brother.

But why?

Why do this to me?

My dad was not really involved.

In truth, I do not know what their motivations were.  Are.

I imagine it stemmed from love.

I imagine it came from concern, compassion.

My sister used to tell me I talked to myself.

Was she right?

Was I missing something major?

I have no choice but to give them the benefit of the doubt.

Crazy.

Violent.

Who was who on what side of the divide?

We were all crossing the river.

Together.

And each to his or her own boat.

We are still crossing the river.

Including my father.

## Chapter 20

I write out of hope.

To give hope.

There are escapes.

There are ways out.

Imagine yourself free.

You will be free.

I am free.

If caught at the crosscurrent of a confluence of tides.

Pulling.

Pulling at me.

Like the moon at the shore.

"Face like the moon," Gen Dikyi la would say.

I am split.

I am fractured.

I will never be whole.

Too many pieces.

Visualize yourself at peace.

Golden silver light streaming in over your shoulder, melting like liquid gold on the lake/ocean/river's surface.

Deceptive? True?

Imagine yourself a part of that light.

Holding fast to your dreams...

...releasing them into the future.

We are all stars connected like myriad points of light in the sky, approaching each other like flames seeking the warmth of comfort in knowing the other person. We recognize each other. Love each other. Reach out to each other. All in the midnight sky-evacuated-black. We, pinpoints of light, know in our souls that we were meant to exist like this. Forever.

## Chapter 21

The snow outside reflected the numbness of the hospital's icy interior. Cambridge Hospital. Teams of doctors, nurses, aids, security...

"Hold still, Jennifer," the officer grabbed my leg and held it firm. The female nurse injected me with a needle. More medicine. "No more pills for you." No trust. "You would not take them if we gave them to you."

Needles.

"Here's a book that will make you feel better," the lawyer recommended. They could not get me discharged. I kept fighting. For two months. Until I started to become a drain on their system, and it was cheaper to release me to the family than keep me on. She recommended *The Center Cannot Hold: My Journey Through Madness* by Elyn R. Saks. The story, apparently, related to mine. (I had a story? Somehow that was not good news.) It was the tale of a university Professor of Law and Psychiatry who had been fighting to be taken off medicine. OK. She pursued it from every angle imaginable from medical to legal. She ended up on medicine. Hmmm...

Books.

"You were looking in my area!" I was. Somebody had stolen the pair of glasses with a faint blue rim. $200.00. Nancy was pissed off. She had been on crack and was now on methadone. I may have the drug name and its antidote wrong. I was not interested.

Fights.

Clothing exchanges. Book exchanges. Story exchanges. Annie was a Harvard graduate student suffering from what appeared to me like withdrawal. I did not notice. She looked fine to me. As she described it, she retreated into an internal world and did not associate with people on the outside. Her boyfriend put her there. Same story with Sarah. Sarah had moved from California to Boston to market her business idea: an envelope for gum she called gumvelope. Or something like that. She stopped interacting with the world for two days. Her boyfriend put her there. She lost custody of her child upon being institutionalised. Who (or what) were we threatening?

Friendships.

Allison. A way out. The occupational therapist who only had positive things to say about me. Her reports ensured I would be let outta there.

The doctors were allied against me. But eventually they had to let me go. They had all sorts of names for me. Schizophrenic. Delusionally paranoid. Bi-polar. Psychotic. Undifferentiated. Differentiated. I'm sure they loved me too.

Escapes.

And then I went from 94 pounds to 123 pounds at which point Dr. Beck probably felt comfortable letting me out. Dr. Gilman was an a--hole according to the social worker, Melanie, who was working on my case. So she involved the head of the unit, Dr. Beck. They were all fighting for something. I was fighting for me.

An EMT lawyer took on my case about legal guardianship. I fought to keep Dr. brother's grubby hands off me. In the end, I had to sign a document insuring that the mother would take over my finances if anything ever happened to me; that is, if I died, was hospitalised, effectively disappeared. What did I have to lose? I had no money. Not even a coin under my tongue. And I would be dead.

Discharge.

It was not until three years later that I discovered that those who did not voluntarily commit themselves to institutions were considered real loonies (the straitjacket and restraints types). I realized I fell into the category. I wanted it on record that I did not volunteer to be manhandled, pincushioned, nor medicated. That's why it is involuntary.

Insanity.

Did I ever feel like I was going to die?

Only the second time the family called the enforcements on me. The time they strapped me to a board, and I could not breathe.

When alone, I was working. Working on enlightenment. I knew I was about to discover something, but that there was a gestation time I had to get through. Every time the family entered the scene, I was about to have a breakthrough. Medicine calls it a psychotic episode. There was greatness on the other side. I could see reality as it really existed. Skeletons walking. Communication without words. No need to eat. To defecate. All bodily processes conserved. A perfect working system. Absolute knowing.

Knowing.

What could be more safe? Provide a greater sense of security? Knowing.

Which is why it is probably considered immoral. Why Eve was vilified for wanting it, and she and Adam were kicked out of the garden of Eden for it. Once you know, it does not matter any more. You could be living in hell and still know the truth. Knowledge is peace.

Stand up for what you know!

Fight!

I live with a thin veil.

Medicine.

It protects as much as it bars my view (protects others from me?). (What threat do I pose?)

It allows me to know as much as anyone can know about me.

In death, we become pinpoints of light. There are no veils in the blackness that envelopes us. Our lights guide us to each other in the darkness.

Love.

Cambridge Hospital was misery. Two months of white sheets, white walls, regulated meals, regulated showers, regulated activities, regulated medicines, regulated contacts with the outside world. Hyper-regulation. A societal disease.

Regulate the banks, don't regulate me!

I'm still fighting. I can see.

## Chapter 22

Which is why I am not ready to write this book.

I'm still looking for enlightenment - a superior view of all that has happened to me so that I may narrate it into a singular, cohesive, sense-ridden story. (A story is a bad thing to have so I want to disguise it in dialogue).

Slavery is a story.

The holocaust is a story.

It means you have to justify your existence. Not fair. It is a survival tactic of the weak. The dominated. Somehow if we can rationalize, justify, explain our oppressors, we will be free. So I will sublimate the story into Art. Somehow that is more noble. Music, poetry. Stories are for children. They are disciplining tools. Morality plays. Lessons.

But to write like a child. That is Art.

Innocence. Purity. Honesty.

So, I want to say, in a non-childlike way, Mom, you suck. Dad, you suck for letting mom get away with it. Dan, I don't blame you. You were caught in a whirlwind just like the rest of us. Liz and Erica, I still have not forgiven you for sending me to the hospital the second time. You were and are complicit.

If I skip the processing part, I know you are guiltless too. Caught in the same whirlwind that Dan and I were caught in. It's a big Chertow-Gregory mess.

Love.

And the story does not end there. It goes on forever.

How many segmentations do we/you need to clarify the order of events?  There are too many to keep track of, and so I will just continue.

## Chapter 23

How did you end up in power? In control of me and my destiny?

My gripes with my parents/family are real.

I admit I once told the other graduate students at an orientation to the department at Stanford that I had a bad family, and

they were my new family.

It seemed to go over well. Though nobody mentioned what I had said to me. Taboo?

I said it.

I no longer think that my family is bad. Just struggling. Like any other family. To make sense of the world.

It is a legacy.

A Chertow-Gregory mess.

Scared

to

name.

"Too many secrets," my brother-in-law, Ahmed from Morocco, once said at a family dinner.

How did he know?

It was none of his business.

There were too many secrets.

I needed them.

That was my secret to success.

Harvard undergrad.  Stanford grad.

University of Chicago in between.

Aaachhh!  What

does

it

matter?

We are all godforsaken.

Death is close.

I

can

feel

it.

It presses on my skin

like a lover.

Hovering.

Pressing...

But I can still breathe.

Unlike the second ambulance ride.

Crossing the river.

Ferrymen taking their pay in any way they can get it.

## Styx

A coin under the tongue.

Enough!

## Chapter 24

"I do not sue!  I do not sue!  I do not sue!"  My new mantra to ensure that I would not fall prey to the privations of the U.S. legal system.

They escorted me out of the ambulance and into the hospital where the police force arrayed itself, and the doctor ("I already had sex with you!"  He was Chinese and reminded me of Roland.   (Another name...)) sedated me.

"Hi-ho! Hi-ho!" Little munchkins morph into dwarves. "It's-off-to-work-we-go!"

## Chapter 25

Cousin Jack committed suicide two days ago.

How?

He jumped off the sixth floor balcony of the condo in Sea Isle City.

My childhood second home.

Shore, beach, breezes, seagulls, ocean into infinity.

Maybe that's what drove him at last to do it.

"Myriad diamonds, Jennifer." "Those are myriad diamonds," my grandmother used to say to me as we looked out at the Atlantic off the balcony,

sun reflecting in-so-many-broken-pieces

off the water.

I loved the seashore,

the boardwalk,

the scents,

the smells,

the joy.

Pizza bagels.

Funnel cakes.

The boardwalk.

And best of all, the haunted house at the end of the boardwalk. Part of the amusement park with a Tilt-O-

Whirl.  Any children growing up during the 1970s who visited the boardwalk know what I'm talking about.  We weren't alone.

After all.

You know what we/I mean.

Well, I still love the boardwalk and the specific condo (The Spinnaker).

There!

I named it.

And I would run off in the opposite direction and go body surfing in the shore.  Rent a boogie board, a raft, anything so that I could be free.

## Chapter 26

Water.

It's hard to describe what water means to me.  I am afraid of it.

But I

love

it.

I grew up swimming in the surf, pools, lakes.  And became very good at it.

State

finalist.

National

qualifier.

Championship

meet

goer.

But I always had/have a healthy fear of water.  I know that's probably how I'm going to die - drowning.

So I am afraid of water as much as I swim in it - even today - three, four times a week - piling up the yardage. Yes, girlfriends, I am over 6000 yards at a time these days.  I made it back to the college tallies/workouts.

I can't do doubles like I used to, but 6000 yards.  That's pretty good, even for me, if I have to say so myself.

I love/hate swimming.  When I'm doing it, I'm doing it. When I'm not doing it, I see the insanity of it.

Up and back.

Follow the black line.

Like a hamster caught on an ever-spinning wheel in its cage, thinking it's getting somewhere when it's really just spinning its wheels.

"I'm a swimmer!"  I screamed/explained.  Dr. Beck replied, "I knew you had me."

I did not know what he meant.

I'm sure

he

did not

know what I meant.  So I explained.  "I swam competitively in high school and college.  I'm a swimmer." I was explaining my weight loss.

They discharged me that day.

They needed something.

But I love swimming.

I needed something.

My mom gave it to me.

A proper meal at the Harvard Club of Boston (I was the member (officially) not my mom) (she paid the dues).

# Styx

Candle light, veal saltimbocca, pasta, service. I was treated like a queen. They do my head too much. Who the hell was I? Why should waiters be serving me? What right...?

And/but I felt special. Well treated after two months of starvation.

There was colour. That's what I remember the most.

Colour.

At the hospital, everything was white. The sheets, the snow. And grey/steel. The needles, the sky.

Here, though the colours did not suit me, too drab, too dark, burgundy and browns, golds and dark greens, there were at least colours.

I needed vivid colours. Turquoise, fuschia, magenta, sea foam green. I'd have to create those on my own.

I couldn't rely on mom for that. How could she know? She knew what she loved. Royal colours.

And we slept at that rich hotel. I forget the name now. But it was rich. Two double beds. And quiet.

I loved myself.

The rest of it was just a storm passing by.

## Chapter 27

Names, names, names. How many names can I remember? I've got them all stored somewhere.

## Chapter 28

Black.

I forgot black.

The colour (is it a colour?), shade, penetrates both inside and outside.  Hard to differentiate, sometimes,

where

I

am

vis-a-vis black.

## Chapter 29

There's more to say.  I just don't know what it is.

I'll end for now.

My favorite trip to India was the one prior to pre-dissertation research.  Because I met Sameera's family; witnessed a Hindu wedding (decorated for it as well); was privy to the work of a video-environmental non-governmental organization; visited Calcutta by train, Madras by train, Bangalore by train, Dharamsala by bus; ate Bengali sweets, fish, butter chicken, Southern Indian vegetarian fare, masala dosa; visited friends from Chicago originally from Bengal; soaked in the sounds, smells, sensations of crowded streets, bright sunny rooftops, late night parties, musical events, street theatre, dramas, dance; met Gayatri Spivak at Seagull Publication's opening (she'd never remember me); held hands; touched; grew affectionate; kissed; slept in; wrote my M.A. thesis; discussed jazz in Delhi, and recovered from what I do not know but left feeling re-invigorated after years of not-living.

We visited Mother Theresa's orphanages, the zoo, the ocean, parks, clean-up projects, old colonial buildings, the computer capital of India, Anglo-Indian districts, Sameera's grade school, high school, the emporium, the bazaar, her cousins, aunts, uncles, sibling, former lover (the Anglo-Indian, Carol, for whom Sameera eventually left me),  relatives all over India.

It was scattered but all of a piece.

One India, ten thousand dialects.

A million sensations.

Sensual, visceral, hot, sweaty, air conditioned, fanned, breezy, stultifying, beautiful. I did preliminary research on torture, human rights, and refugees in Dharamsala. There I met Mr. Dorjee who worked for Tenzin Choedrak, the late personal physician to the Dalai Lama. Mr. Dorjee gave me a book by Alexandra David-Neel and asked if I would be willing to organize a trip for Tenzin Choedrak. Ecstatic that I would be picked out of the myriad tourists coming to the area, I agreed and promised to do what I could to facilitate a Chicago trip.

Sameera met me in Dharamsala.

We stayed at a German-run hostel with an Ohm sign just outside its wooden entrance. The lodgings were sparse but the price was right and with body heat, the temperature was too. It felt a sacrilege to be together with Sameera in a place I considered so holy, sacrosanct, in my mind, on a mission I felt should be as pure as possible ("I feel so clean!" she exclaimed one night after making love in Evanston. Her comment always disturbed me.) academic as it was.

Nothing could beat India in the winter. It was a welcome (much needed) respite. From what, I do not know. But it was an escape I forced myself to take in order to sustain a relationship that was doomed from the start. I loved Sameera. She came after the first long term relationship I had ever had. A three year doozey with sex, drugs and rock-and-roll. With a summa-cum-laude Harvard graduate, Bill, a year older than I. Bill and I travelled all over together. The U.S., Southeast Asia, South Asia.

Surface travelling, I call it.

Because we never really delved beneath the surface.

It was a mélange of lonely-planet cultures all packaged into one for the time-constrained traveller looking for the (cheap) "authentic" in the everyday. It/he got me interested in graduate work. Making love in Indonesian thatched-hut rice paddies. The act itself a validation of a world we did not know, understood at a surface level, and wanted to consecrate. Fried banana toast sandwiches (surprise!) awaited us in the mornings, cool showers awaited us in the evenings, shadow puppets, street music, and Hindu gods filled our days and nights.

We revelled.

We were young-in-love.

A beautiful relationship.

I still dream about Bill. Feel our soul. We experienced a lot (the world) together. During those post-graduate years.

Here, I have to stop.

## Chapter 30

"She had a homosexual relationship with a woman!" "Don't you think that could be part of her being sick!" my mom screamed/explained to the psychiatrist who originally took me on as a patient upon my return from India the third time. He never said a word.

Linking homosexuality to psychiatric disorders was so passé.

## Chapter 31

Our love was deep. It stemmed from a well-spring of trust. I absolutely trusted Bill. He would never cheat. He encouraged my engineering prowess at Jinga. I actually had a crush on his best friend, Eric, who always seemed to be making fun of me (and who was with Cathy).

[Eric studied medicine and pharmacology at the University of California, San Francisco. He was brilliant. And into drugs. As was Bill. As was I, for a short time, is that why I got sick? And making brew. The two of them, distilling, fermenting, tasting. All in San Francisco. A stressful, free, time of life.

Jogging in Golden Gate park.

Feeling the Ocean Beach breeze on my face.

Surf.

Sand.

It was wilder than New Jersey. Craggy cliffs dropping off into the ocean. Violent waves pounding the shore.

Asia faced east.

Europe west.

We looked them dead in the eyes across those oceans.]

It was a swinging lifestyle without all the swinging. And too many drugs. Not that I did them. I was studying "South Asia" at Berkeley. Working as a temp worker in the city. With the gay guy/instructor/doctor. At least not all that often.

## Chapter 32

I can tell my life stops upon entrance into graduate school at Stanford.

Another river to be crossed at another time.

I get burned from memories that are too close.

Too sacred.

Too far away.

Too taboo.

I remember the day my mom came to pick me up from Stanford.

It was a blustery day in San Francisco, but Palo Alto was temperate. Mom wanted to see San Francisco.

We drove to Coit Tower. Took pictures of the murals painted during the post-depression era. It foreshadowed today's recession. All those muscular working bodies.

Tilling the land.

Building highways.

Working in factories.

The mining tragedies of today an echo of tragedies past.

All for the sake of the country.

Workers of the world unite!

It was/is the most socialist time.

Frugal.

Sparse.

Golden yellow and brown.  Red.

We ended up at the seafood restaurant she loved (I forget the name) and drank lemon drops, wine, water, martinis and ate linguini with clams; that's all I can remember.  That and all the boxes we shipped out of the United Postal Service that afternoon (before Coit) (I had had them organized so as to prevent my mother from suffering/having to pack).

I was coming off the medicine at that time.  I knew

she was worried.

I was

worried.

Which was why I had her come out to get me.  They take away your self-sustenance.

Freedom?

Everything else is a blur until I submitted the dissertation three months later; four months before the second hospitalisation/official graduation date.

Graduation, we (the family) celebrated a year earlier when I originally thought I would be outta there (another institution).

I walked.

In my white-and-pale-green-trimmed Armani Exchange dress with my Tibetan doctor friend, Yangdron Kalzang, by my side feeding me dumplings.  The whole family showed up.

I was so proud!

We visited the Stanford Linear Accelerator (Ju Gao, my engineer-room mate from Guangdong Province, recommended that one), Santa Cruz, the boardwalk, crab houses, piers, Ghirardelli Square where we imbibed hot fudge sundaes and stocked up on chocolate for the rest of the year and my dad.

No expense was too much. They stayed at the Sheraton. $3000.00. (Mom paid.) Where we had brunch the next day, and Drue Kataoka was "dramatic" but endearing.

I loved my family. (They were there to celebrate me!) They do my head too much...

The transition to Evanston was as hard as the transition back to the U.S. after returning from Tibet. Power struggles, jockeying for position, who was in control of what? (I was a PhD. dammit!).

But who cares.

That's not

the point.

I got lost in there somewhere/how.

Too many confluences/currents.

Tides.

I was in control. Erica was in control. Mom was in control. Dad was the boss. As I tried to explain at my sister's baby shower not two weeks ago, "Liz is in charge," "I'm in charge," "We're all in charge." The guests laughed (I did not know I was funny) (Don't people laugh when they're nervous?).    Our public display of dysfunction.

And so I teeter, stolidly, on this fragile, massive house

balancing

like

a

ballerina.

Pirouetting throughout the sky, leaving a trail of circles behind me.  It's all a beautiful act/

show.

## Chapter 33

This future book is part of that act/show. Which is why I am not ready to write it. Because it is meant to be solid ground. A jumping off point. A show stopper. A conversation starter. A piece de resistance!

Does it fall short?

Surpass the goal?

I love myself.

Crazy!

## Chapter 34

Yet another memory

floods in (I feel like Sethe).

Keila Diehl and I attended the invite-only (the former representative of the Dalai Lama to the U.S. (I forget his name) had invited Stanford-Friends-of-Tibet, and we were included on the list) talk of the Dalai Lama to Muslim religious leaders in San Francisco. I had already seen the Dalai Lama give a Heart Sutra talk at Shoreline Amphitheatre in Mountain View a few years earlier. He came to Stanford again not a year before to sanction the beginning of a Tibet Studies programme, which I had suggested many years earlier.

Keila wanted to offer a white scarf to the Dalai Lama. I did not. It was not the appropriate time or place. That much I had learned after being hospitalised in/kicked out of India (the zero-ith time I was hospitalised). She did not understand. I stopped her. We sat at a window in the Mark Hopkins Hotel facing the side of the audience that faced the Dalai Lama. And listened. Nothing new. Peace. Compassion. Wisdom. Love. And I could see Keila mouth to herself (was it sarcastic? Defiant?) "I love myself."

## Chapter 35

Black.

The colour that is not a colour that indicates and erases boundaries.

## Chapter 36

We were two white girls (she whiter than I) too innocent to know the rules. The purity of our intentions surely matched that of the Dalai Lama.

Who cares?

Why compare?

Not my business.

Really.

"Ngai chutok med." ("It's not my business.") Young women and old would approach me in the streets of Lhasa and spit/whisper the phrase to me under their breaths.

I never knew what they meant.

Not until this future book when I will decipher all meanings.

I can't wait to find out.

Even though I know I will have to make it up.

The phrase refers to death and violence.

What else could it be?

They knew. And they knew I knew until I could not possibly know.

Whew! That's a doozey. That must be what they meant.

I was medicine free at the time. So I must have had some insight into the situation.

**Styx**

Just as I am medicine-ridden now and must riddle through the situation.

It is crazy.

## Chapter 37

Boudhanath Temple.

Nepal.

Holy site.

Buddhist centre.

Sarah and I had gone to Nepal to renew our visas for our stay in Tibet. She wanted to stay at Boudhanath. I followed. What did I care?

The monk in the room next to mine at Pema Tashi's Guesthouse had a cute little white dog that yapped when you/I approached. I spent many afternoons in that monk's room learning what he was doing there, why he had a dog, where he planned to travel. The Rinpoche and disciple that Sarah knew were transporting gold Buddha statues over the border. Nawang later told me about the elaborate smuggling scheme of gold over borders. I'm sure these monks had nothing to do with that. I guess/hope.

The guest house owners spent afternoons in front of a large T.V. watching Hindi videos - Bollywood fare - in the dark, no sunlight. I wanted to watch, too, and could not understand why they wanted to sit in the dark. Instead, I travelled into Kathmandu with Sarah to eat bread at German bakeries, write in my journal, and collect the visa.

"Jen, the United States just got attacked! Come on over; it's on T.V."

"What are you talking about?"

"Two tall buildings in New York...the World Trade Center... Two planes flew into the buildings..."

"Oh my god! I'm coming right over."

I had no T.V. in my room. It was near midnight. I gathered a few things together, a flashlight, and went to the Rinpoche's house where Sarah was staying.

We stayed up all night watching the horrible footage of planes crashing into buildings, listening to reports of planes crashing into the Pentagon, a field in Pennsylvania (phew...at least one did not make it to a landmark - go passengers!). Numbed, we flew into Lhasa two days later. Blessed that we were not in the U.S.

I remained for two years. More holy sites. Pilgrimages. Chinese/Tibet.

I felt more isolated than I ever had in my entire life.

Days filled with phone calls from/meetings with friends. All Tibetan, mostly from Lhasa. They knew more about where they had come from than I could ever hope to know; so they showed me around, explained things, fed me, entertained me, and mostly befriended me.

Stark landscapes increased the feeling of isolation. Dry, brown plateaus; sky-climbing peaks; dust-ridden roads; and a sky that went on into forever. An escape. Looking into myriad stars above; hundreds of constellations. I knew I was free.

I felt acted upon rather than an actor in the world.

But I was in love with the idea that I could do whatever I wanted in the world - even travel and live in Tibet.

So I would endure it.

Love.

## Chapter 38

"Shimiiiiiii!" screamed the opponent on the Tibetan-police-force soccer team. "Prostitute!!!" was the direct translation. I had picked up soccer as a form of exercise with the Japanese and Korean students at Tibet University (the name!). I had no clue how to play but had been an athlete so picked up the game quickly. Not quickly enough because the taunt sent me flying after the soccer ball to prove I was not a "shimi" and over the curb at the edge of the soccer field. I heard a pop and a tear.

An emergency room visit and an x-ray later (at the People's No. 1 Hospital) confirmed it was a bad sprain and not broken, but I was bed-ridden for nearly a month trying to recover from the accident. Maria went out and got me crutches. She brought me food and stayed by my side for a week. Sarah had gone by then.

I had made new friends.

Escapes, exits, outs. Tibet represented all of that to lots of residents.

## Chapter 39

An administrator at the Lhasa Municipal Hospital and I hit off a great friendship. I tutored her son, half-Tibetan/half-Chinese, in English. She provided me with interview subjects for the research, namely her mother. She (the mother) lauded the presence of the Chinese in Tibet, explained why the one-child policy worked, and why contraception was a modern miracle-wonder. Nobody wanted trouble with the Chinese.

Today those experiences are present just as much as they are distant. I maintain contact with two Tibetan friends, Tsam la (the research assistant on the project I conducted) and Jampa Dolkar (a former worker at the Lhasa Hotel (previously the Holiday Inn) who now works as a taxi-lender. Neither job was more glamorous than the next.) Others come into and out of consciousness when a renegade e-mail makes its way to me. "Tashi Delek! I hope you and your family are well" from Pasang Tsering of One Heart or Kalsang Dikyi of the MacFarlane Burnet Project now under the auspices of Australia-AID. Nawang is from Chicago. Originally from Nepal. Originally, originally from Tibet. Like I'm originally, originally from Russia, Poland and Italy.

Crazy.

## Chapter 40

And so now I prepare to become an M.D. Medical school is a year away if all goes as planned. In the meantime, I work at Northwestern University. My colleagues are great! Very personable, open, friends. Sometimes we go out in the city. To bars, coffeehouses, restaurants, music venues.

Jenny fills the gap when I need an escape.

She and I grew up together in Evanston, sailing at Aquatic Camp, getting stalked by mentally unstable older men. "The girl with the prominent nose" - a letter left at the front door of the house where I lived just down the street from the beach. Scared out of our minds, we crouched in the upper floors and looked down as he left his missive. Then, captured by the police, an investigation uncovered his unstable, halfway-house roots. Whew! The letter was not meant for me - Jenny had the prominent nose (though I never said anything).

Scary.

It reminded me of an incident much earlier in childhood. I walked down the block avoiding the glass in bare feet when I ran into a group of men, one of whom was peeing against a stone wall.

"Come here little girl," he beckoned.

I bolted like a flash back to the house. Never would I go to the beach to meet the parents alone again. Only together. As a family.

## Chapter 41

The race was exhilarating. I stood on the block. The screams of the crowd pounding in my ears. Never before had I been a part of such excitement. How could all the people, witnesses, be so present!? Their voices carried me off the block. I placed top ten in the 50 free. At New Trier (our rivals). Giving us 9th place overall at state. At 14 years old what more could I ask for?

Except the perversion of the coach, which did not reveal itself (thankfully never to me personally) until six months later when it came out that he had slept with a fifteen year old student, derisively referred to by unsympathetic peers as Amy "Ho" Fosch. Police were called in. Statutory rape. Child pornography charges. Divorce. Fatherless children. Jail. And a marriage between Amy Fosch and her teacher when Amy was of age to prevent Sheehan (the name!) from going to jail. The last bit of the rumour was hearsay, which I could confirm if I cared to.

Hell! What an a--hole.

## Chapter 42

Which is why I am still not ready to write this book. Because I am still fighting.

"Lay 'em down, Sethe. Sword and shield. Down. Down. Both of 'em down..."

## Chapter 43

Sometimes poetry penetrates our psyches, fulminates there, and releases images, words, thoughts never before spoken. That is the work of Art. To which I aspire. Childlike. This is the beginning. The middle as a place of initiation.

Christ!

I wish I had some way of getting across the soul.

To you, dear reader.

So you could see some of yourself unfractured and whole.

A replacement of the Lacanian mirror.

Crazy!

But it only brings pain.

Truth.

Hell.

The work is in the working. Peace. Intelligence. Wisdom. Compassion. It is all of a piece. One cloth. Wrapping. Wrapped.

Blood

soaked.

Sweat

soaked.

I do not cry.

Not for Africa.

Not for me.

The wisdom of the world awaits me like an open shell.

I remember the baobab trees.

Poking

against the sky.

And myriad stars overhead glistening down on our foreheads, my sister(s) and I sleeping beneath the stars.

Heat rising from the earth, warming us in the cool night air.

Nangadef!

White, white Touba with magnificent mosques.

Clean.

Clear.

Beautiful.

Night dancing.

And discotheques.

It was a whirlwind.

Flash to Greece.

White buildings stark against the Mediterranean, indigo infused sky.

Turquoise.

Striking. Death.

And figurines/people affixed in black frozen lava. Pompeii. Mouths agape, caught in mid-scream.

The Algarve. Lisbon. Golden blue beaches. Art.

Gaudi in Barcelona.

Architecture, buildings, landmarks, hostels, homes.

Structure structuring existence.

The list goes on.

The centre does not hold.

Boat rides, ferries, trains, buses, automobiles, bicycles...

Bicycling through Kyoto to visit myriad tombs, temples, sacred gardens existing in perfect symmetry. Leaving my bags locked in the train station for a day's ride through the city. Shinkansen transporting me (bullet train) back to Tokyo.

To a friend. His one room apartment and a home-cooked meal. We hit all the fashion spots in the city. Met Yi. Exchanged contact information. Loved.

Kyoto shadows of fog rising in a mist on the stairs built so civilly into mountainsides leading to markets, bazaars and carnivals.

Spirited Away! (Another name!)

## Chapter 44

Black.

It keeps coming back.

## Chapter 45

And the world opens like an oyster. Venus rising from its foaming shell. The Birth of Venus! Botticelli had us.

Who do we have?

Swimming. Night swimming.

Naked.

Nude as the day I was born.

As a baby's bottom.

The words/phrases

meanings

are fitting

together.

There is a point.

Love.

Immersed in love

immersed in love.

Like a double chocolate dipped strawberry.

Sensations, sensual, free.

The future book is almost (beginning-wise) done.

Because we started in the middle.

Popped it in the oven to see if it would cook.

# Chapter 46

It's still raw, and so I'm still not ready to write.

Create your own book!  This one's mine.

Distillates and all.

## Chapter 47

Smoking. 7 cigarettes in a row. That's what I remember most about Turkey. That and the abscesses I got under my armpits from shaving in dirty water (I had one surgically incised upon the return to Evanston), swimming in the Black Sea, sand, pollution.

Cozy, hot, smoky coffeehouses. Dr. Gezer (a colleague of the mom) had relatives, who kindly took me in and told my future in the bottom of Turkish coffee cups. And tried to convert me to Islam. And loved me. I loved them, too, but I would not convert.

Merhaba!

He always reminds me of how I had been swimming in the Black Sea when two young Turkish men came to my rescue and recovered the diamond ring (a graduation present from my aunt) from the brackish waters.

I always remember how, when I landed on Turkish shores, Ephesus, from Lesbos (I had to go to Lesbos - the Greeks had a term for female-female love that fit into their ancient cosmology! (souls)), a young Turkish boy/man approached me, offered me a ride to a (his) hotel, and saw me off the next day on an air-conditioned bus to Ankara, translating on my behalf all the while. Ataturk had a vision. Modern Turkey wins!

Peace camp was on the shores of the Black Sea. Capitalist industrialist homes on the seafront. Red tomatoes, feta and black olives every morning for breakfast. One week for $200.00.

Byzantine temple restoration amounted to a tourist visit to caves with broken relics in them. They (the capitalist/power-mongering mayor) directed us to painting bike lanes instead. Factories belched black smoke out onto lush green landscapes.

We got lost on a trip down to the shore from a high, leafy ledge. Turned out to be a sewage outlet into the sea. We hailed a passing fishing boat, waded into the water, and hitched a ride back (swimming off the boat en route) to Izmit near Zonguldak.

Brussels offered a welcome respite from Mediterranean life. French, mussels, chocolates, clean hostel bed (four to a room)

[(six to a room - until I found Poacher's Inn with medium-clean singles) in Beijing; 3 Yuen bus trips into to Tiananmen Square (Mao all over the place), the Forbidden City (Bertolucci's *Last Emperor* come to life), the Summer Palace (Empress Dowager's vacation spot), and a token Tibetan chorten.

These trips invigorated and exhausted me to the point that I was happy to return to the U.S. and work as a temp worker in my mom's office correcting grants for her boss, whose wife she despised; teach English to Bosnians coming to the U.S. from a war-torn Yugoslavia; contemplate grad school. I hated that job.]

and a central square with a clock tower that marched figures out every hour on the hour and every half hour.

Bill. I think of you.

**Addendum**

"You ain't got nuthin'..."

Prison inmate to prison inmate in Lady Gaga's video *Telephone*.

<u>Chapters</u>

## Chapter 48

Some things might never be written.  Too painful to share.

Humiliating.

Horrifying.

De-humanising.

Stolen.

Embarrassing.

Right now, I want to focus on the stolen.

It is nobody's right but your own to impute meaning according to your own world view.

Not have it appropriated to fit someone else's world view, logic, end.

Like that damned EMT lawyer did.

With MY story (I apologize for the capitals, but they are necessary).

I threw the cup at her, the nurse.

And no, it did not have pee in it.

And yes, I did not want her to come in.

They were checking.

Checking for hydration.  Sugar.  Pee levels.

I shut the door on her.

It was my privacy.

Nobody,

my humanity,

should

take

away

the

one

moment

of

privacy

in

a

ripple

effect

of

events

infringing

on

my...

Nothing.

No words.

## Styx

Nothing.

Horrifying.

And

so

I

fought,

physically.

Barred the door.

Wrestled the sample from her hands

and dumped

it

back

into

the

toilet

so that

she

could

not

examine.

Look.

Taste.

Test.

Evaluate.

Contemplate.

Surmise.

Gesticulate.

And decide.

"It's all in the urine!  Proof of her psychosis!"

No thank you.

Not for me.

I wouldn't want to taste it.

He raped my insight.  That EMT lawyer.

A--hole.

## Chapter 49

And so I know I am not ready to write.


There.

I

spat

it

out.

## Chapter 50

It goes back to the beginning. That pre-first hospitalisation. The

one

in

India.

Where I refused to take the pill.

I spat it out,

and

they forced

me

to

take

it again.

No fair.

# Chapter 51

The

Indian

lady

forcing

me

to

take

pills

(and

then

give

me

shots)

was

crazy.

Why

would

you

do

that

to

someone?

Really.

It's

an

honest

question.

There was nothing wrong with me.

Honestly.

Stick-a-needle-in-my-eye.

She had nothing.

"You ain't got nuthin'..."

Phew!  I can still write.

## Chapter 52

Beijing gardens. Mist-laden. Damp. Soul-place. Tourists wandering purposefully (?) around the garden. Nobody could see us in our mute pantomimes.

Of humanity.

What did we know?

What the hell did we know?

Double chocolate, my ass.

This is torture.

Genuine pain.

Numb tears.

Why doesn't anybody understand?

Why

does-

n't

an-

y

bo-

dy

un-

der-

stand?

It's too stupid.

Just a hug would help.

Honestly.

Judy.

(you earned a place in the narrative!)

Christ.

I wish I didn't have to swear.

God doesn't appreciate it.

## Chapter 53

Stop.

Go.

Turn left.

Turn right.

Turn back.

Cover your steps.

Cover your paces.

Cover your tracks.

Hide!

There is no escape.

## Chapter 54

I tried.

I got away for a moment and headed straight for the green-light door.

Where would I go?

Out.

Into the night.

Back into the night

To the apartment.

Mealy-stuffing-infested place.

Wewerewalkingtothenextunit.

I knew what was coming.

But they,

police/Dr. brother,

caught me by the collar.

Stopped.

Me.

Injected me with myriad needles.

Medicine.

Relief.

It was over.

## Styx

The-

scene-

had-

been-

played-

out.

# Chapter 55

Skip!

**Addendum II**

**Chapter 56**

I am not ready to write this future book.

I think it's over before it's even begun. This future book.

There's an infinite amount more to say.

Broken narrative...

Reality. Nobody's seen the insides of a psychotic episode. The narrative brings you as close to the harrowing truth as possible. A reflective account. A piecing together. Quilt-like. Made of blood and bones. It's body matter. The process is slow. Painstaking. Dust motes travelling from the past into the future, carrying bits of me with them. Each step toward the future is a battle against the past. Its ripping grip. Shaping us in ways we do not want to be shaped. A master sculptor, the past. But I do not like my impression there. My eye there. Or my lip there. The whole figure. And so I fight against the past to shape my present/future. The material itself. The stuff of which I am made. Dust. Water. Colour. Sienna red. Coal black. Turquoise blue. Sea foam green. Magenta purple.

## Chapter 57

Visualizing the future. Filling the void. Black into stars. Nebula rising. Soul enchanting. Expanding. Beautiful. Whispering in my ear. Soft words of love. Caring. Tenderness. Loved.

Fulfilling dreams. Fulfilling my vision. Sailing out to sea. On golden sea-foam, green waters. Into forever. Wrapping the horizon around her shoulders.

I.

I alone.

Through this devastation, struggle, fight.

Why do they want to kill me?

Save me?

Don't they have it confused?

It is a plea to stop the pain. They, Dr. brother and the rest, are causing the pain.

I no longer know.

Skip!

Flip!

There is no return from the abyss, the other side, hades.

## Chapter 58

I return.

Sound. Whole. Of a piece. Whisking away on the wind. I'm just not interested. Can't entice me.

Other-side-in. Blisk. Misk. Isk. I chant. Chaos.

An abyss. Vacuum. Before. (Never never land.)

That is where I lived for 10 years in 11 months - Slipping, they say, into an increasingly psychotic state, isolating/floating, I say, into a mystic peace. Solace in...sanctuary in...bless them, that godforsaken apartment, a death place, a hide-away. They left me alone. Thank god alone. Until the intruders came.

What return? What journey? Haven't I been here the whole time? "You were gone so long, Jen. We didn't know who you were any more" the mother exclaims to me. Moments of strangeness. They look foreign to me as well.

Too different.

Which is why the reinsertion is violent. Comfortable. If a lie. Placement is impossible.

Disjuncture.

No space.

Discomfort.

"Move!"

The third/second hospitalisations merge.

Scream!

Is what I meant to say.  Not skip.  Open your mouth and scream!  A quiet circle around your teeth, larynx open, voice box vibrating, scream!

The closer I get to fitting in my silhouette, the greater the dissonance.  Fight the fit because the only thing on the other side is death.  And yet in searching for what?  An escape?  There is only death.  Because there is no escape or, rather, place, and when you find that place - that is death.

Skip! Because

that

is

why

the

mind

splits.

...but names can never hurt me

Peace is in alternate universes.    Out-of-sync simultaneous soul places.    Zero-ith hospitalisation. Infinity realities.

The organization matters.

Must be clear.

Transparent.

Of a piece.

Or else the words ( - and their listeners - ) stop.  And then, there truly is nothing.

Chaos.

## Chapter 59

Which is hope.

And why I am writing this future/present book? Because I think that is the point.

Being nothing permits the world from being born. In toto.

Complete.

Whole.

Without miss.

Just out of reach. Feel. Touch. Barely/nearly tangible. Diaphanous. Evanescent. A gauzy top. The essence of the book.

See-through.

Feel-through.

There-not-there.

Air.

And traces of the material.

Something.

Sitting in the trenches. Bloodied, unused, bayonets in hand. Green and brown. Post-shade. Dark and light. Before. Middle. After.

The decision has been reached.

**Styx II**

**Chapter 60**

Lucid.

Disciplined.

Good girl. Docile. Obedient. Trained.

Counter.

No exit.

Committed.

Love puts me in the madhouse.

Doctors visit. I am convinced they are doing lobotomies on the top floor. And that I am next.

Fear.

Of.

The Unknown.

Death.

Name it, and it goes away. That fear.

Simplicity.

I left the first hospital with my brother. The sunlight, of an unusual quality, bright, golden, afternoon, slanting, glanced off the bed/garden outside the window in the hotel. My brother had rented the room, and I slept there from exhaustion. It was a miracle room. Warm, comforting, lazy.

The plane ride home was filled with monks falling out of the backside of my head (I stopped taking the medicine). Chanting and chanting and chanting. It was the plane's motor-noise. But I meditated the entire flight back.

I walked to the grandparents' house. They answered the door. Maybe 6 miles away. Surprised at my arrival. Calling home. Giving me food/drink. Love. I thought they would take me in. They did and called home anyway.

Mom, dad, and brother came to pick me up. This time, the hospital. They discussed it and discussed it and did not consult me. I volunteered to go to the hospital. I knew they wouldn't hurt me. I went with a bag. I took a shower upon arrival. Steel cold, hot water, black tile, locked door. Soap, shampoo. The next day I felt better. 9 days. They released me when I sculpted the brain out of clay. I counted them. It was time to be discharged.

And then I met the doctor. He listened to the story and said I could chalk it up to being a "religious experience." I cringed at the

patron-

i-

sa-

tion.

They would call it a psychotic break.

I returned to school and got all A's (prove myself!). Taught three courses. Was weaned off the medicine. The doctor (a new one) wanted to be "conservative." It took six months. I counted on it (the episode) being a fluke and continued work. Language training, exams, proposals; they were not ready to let me go. I went.

Then began the Tibet (There, I named it! Gave it away.) era. Hugs upon arrival. System. Organization. Old life started again. Work began. I fitted right in. I knew my place. Guest.

Lift the veil. See what is unseen. Know.

New York. Not Disney. Edge. Not cotton candy. Real. Not representation.

Direct experience.

What other facets of existence could travel offer me?

It was all re-al/-search. Direct experience. A memory. A future projection. La difference? The medicine did not pollute me at the time. Things were "normal." Was my re-ality/-search valid? Tainted? What was real any more?

So confident. So certain. Our epistemology is the platform.

Question.

Pre-

episteme.

Chaos.

Truth.

Before the big bang.

What if before the big bang was now?

Does that make it inside-out?  Inside and out?

There was a time when I did not need permission to be free.  That was before the big bang.

## Chapter 61

Sleep.

There was no time before sleep.  Just waking.

Night merged into day.  The Somerville era.  Pre-third hospitalisation.  Peace.

Nest during day.  Nest during night.

Shop for food.

Register.

Attend lecture.

Distractions from the real purpose.

To gestate.  Merge past into future.

Go where you know.

Regroup.

Prove yourself.

Forces allied against me.

Thwarted.  Emergent.  Hospitalised.

Root shoots ripped from the soil.

Tender, dangling, exposed.

Bribes, lying, stealing.

In a quest for the truth.

No teeth.

Ideation at the seeding of the universe.

Love.

"Wipe your mouth.  No elbows on the table.  No burping." I burped.

No good girl.

Etiquette unravels.

Proof!

Why?

Kiss.

Bare chested, I broke down in tears.  Doctor walked in. Smiled.  Tee-shirt in a pile next to me.  Needle in leg.

Sedated.

Nothing.

Expunge.  Purge.  Excrete.

Circle-spiral.

Like a slinky.

Just keep bouncing back-and-forth.  In a never-ending cycle.  The infinite oscillator.

Black ink.

Doubling back on itself.

Overriding what is written before.

Until all becomes night.

## Styx

Skip! Scream.

No salvation.

Only

struggle.

Respite (fake, not real), here

and there.

Shower steam.

Towels.

Pyjamas clean.

A respite.

Keep on going.

Art. In pictures, words, reading.

Treacherous, traitor movement.

Transition. Theirs/mine.

Bliss. (ters)

on my soul.

I never doubted what they knew.

If they knew. I knew/would know.

In this future book.

Christ.

Summer walks. Snow houses. It all turned grey.

Yellow and red to grey and white.

I lived.

Nothing hurt me.

Train ride.  Sleeper car.  Broken Amtrak trip.

Union Station to South Station.

And trees, fields, buildings in between.

I was tired of flying.

The airport.

Turn on the air dryer.

I hated flying.

No escape.

Trepidation at the terminal.

Hyung loved music.  Sang with it all the time.  Said it drowned out the voices.

I had no voices but sympathized with his need to drown them out anyway.  We hugged as I left.  He found me.

He said his sister was in the U.S.  He said he was Mormon.  I introduced him to the brother when he visited.  He washed dishes in a Korean restaurant for a living.  His mother had abandoned his sister and him. He was not a citizen.  I loved him.

I loved them all.

The fellow patients.

Our bond?

Common bondage.

Locked up.  Kept apart.  Out.

There were no houses for us.

Just approximations.

I remember Hyung.  Late night meetings.  Revelations of the soul.  "You're not stupid." I clarified, "'Group' is stupid."  We all had names on our doors.  She (the nurse) later told me I was not dumb.

I kept projecting my soul hoping someone would catch it.  No one ever did. (Except Bill, except Bill doesn't count).

It was a maligned existence.

All that hate with no object.

Nebulous, murky no-object.

The days pass.  Slowly.  Quickly.  Uneven in their syncopated rhythm.  And I live through them.  That is the story.  "Quanta storia!" My grandmother used to say to me.  "So many stories!"  I always used to translate in my mind or more officially, "How much history!"

A-tonal.

Un-even.

Ir-reverent.

**Book Journal I**

I just had to spew.

Information I deem personal.

It's hate.

Grace should be given.

I should just be forgiven.

It is inappropriate for me to have to make the appeal myself since others put me in the position of having to make the appeal in the first place. Horrifying. This is what I meant by the present impinging on the past - a past I am only beginning to piece together (like a blood and bones quilt). Scear (scare and fear = scar). Through memories, images.

I guess that's all I have to say. The rest is just mundane details. A letter from the psychiatrist in charge of my care after my zero-ith hospitalisation. A letter from the psychiatrist in charge of me during my third hospitalisation. It gives me the shivers. There is something murderous about the institutionalisation. A horror that lurks behind the mask of clinical precision. Logic. It is because I was not on medicine and because I had been put on it in the first place. That is why I had to be hospitalised the second and third time. And I am trying to order it for you. It is all crazy. To prevent it from happening again. So that the world knows the truth. And stop-gaps are put into place to prevent the mistreatment not of patients but of your everyday soul. Not "human" because that has too many un-kosher associations. The concept of "human" is what the holocaust was built upon in the first place. Gen-ocide. "Gen" means people, race.

So, I just keep on writing. In the hope that one day these words will penetrate your soul and lead to a worldwide wave of love - a swelling of love. A dismantling of the system (aspects of it) that creates the conditions for devastation to take place. A small earthquake (pointed, precise, specific) that breaks apart the steel undergirding, insertions, wedges, gaskets, that give rise to edifices of horror. Iron cages. Shifts things ever so slightly so that everyone, simultaneously, gets a whiff of fresh air, a glimpse of sunlight, a shattering of the shade that covers psyches, mental apparatuses, in darkness.

Reverberates throughout every universe. I feel halfway there. Halfway to signifying the horror. So that it can be named and unnamed simultaneously. Dismantled. The point? To emerge.

It is time to emerge. From the cocoon. Though I have not been changing. There is no metamorphosis in this tearing away of facades, fabrics, cottony-gauzy-nylon-fishnet materials. I have merely been gestating. Masticating. Stewing in my skin, bones, blood. Tears, sweat. Waiting to emerge as I was when I was born - clean, unfettered, innocent. I am fighting against the blame, scapegoating, and guilt. It is not our fault. Whatever your problem (and you know who you are), we (the souls) are not to blame. You have just become so alienated from your own soul, that you are seeking other souls to blame for your mis-identification. (See http://en.wikipedia.org/wiki/Social_alienation). Your anomie. (See http://en.wikipedia.org/wiki/Anomie). It's so basic it's stupid. Anybody could tell you what was wrong with you and that you are projecting your own psychic dissonance onto the innocent. I am writing against criminalization, institutionalisation, and anomilisation of souls. This is not a treatise or diatribe on the "mentally insane," or a defense of the "diseased." You, the sufferers of mis-identification, the blamers, are the target of the writing - so that you may save yourselves. Turn your gaze on yourself. Not me. Read a little deconstruction. You may be born again. It will do you good. Identify with yourself. Not me. Or else you will start to blame me again. "Innocent!" I exclaim. "Innocent!" Blame yourself. You are the cause of your own mis-identification. Because you do not recognize the symptoms in society of general anomie and alienation. The disjuncture between the worker, you, and ownership of means/modes of production. The codification. The labelling. The naming. Hint: Un-name yourself, and you will be free. I worked on it myself for a long, long time. And that is part of the revelation. The rest of it is living that way, emerged, from that day forward, every day, every second, millisecond, microsecond, picosecond into infinite divisions of every day of your existence. Or else your only escape is death. And I would hate to be the one to know that and not you - don't shoot the messenger - as I may one day be the bearer of bad news - that you have failed to recognize your mis-identification and so must keep trying lest you die. This is the profound truth I am trying to inform you about, name, signify, indicate, point to, allude to, reference, glancingly, because to "reveal" it, "unveil" it, is to risk insanity/death. While I'm not a huge fan of computerized animation propaganda films, John Cameron's *Avatar* related a smidgeon of this message. Not mine. Yours. I was/was not near death. On the one hand, I was losing weight. Sleeping. Thinning. On the other hand, I was not stupid and knew that to eat was important. That was the role of cabbage. I was purifying my system. Ridding it of medicine. Toxicants. Illness causing/signifying-lactation. And at one point, just to note, - it's ridiculous! if you think about it - cream leaking from my nipples! - apples, though they were less

Styx

important. I took one 2.5 milligram dose of medicine in the middle of my "anorexia nervosa" (that's meant to be a joke), pre-third hospitalisation, gestation period (I still have not emerged but am closer), and started lactating! Now, though I am on medicine and as a result have fear, I enjoy food, though I know it toxifies my system - I realize I cannot fully emerge until I am left alone - 100% - not 90%, 95%, - 100%.

I do not want to be alone. That is not the point. The point is that I do not want to be under the auspices of anybody, my parents, my boyfriend, my girlfriend, anybody, and that is not possible - so in the meantime signifying is the primary point of my existence - once I stop signifying, shudder, horror, enveloping blackness without pinpoints of comforting warmness, light. I want a fabric of support, nylon, that repels water, does not stick but - a mesh of (brilliant) souls - validating the significations I enscript/speak/sing/play/intone. This is the       way-of-life       path/journey/gestation/existence. Toward emerge. Verb-form. (That is a demand not a request.) In order to unstick myself from you. Dad does not know what I am writing about. He is clueless, which is fine because unstick is the (one) way to assert your/my soul. As separate. Buoyed. Floating. Like dust motes drifting in air. Respect is an artifice of society that brings us down. Dragging. Into the abyss. Grandma (Dad's mom) once said, "Too much respect." She was right. My dad has too much respect for me. How can I be free? So I (hope that I won't always have to) fight by giving too much respect back. So there. Snotty little kid "talking"/thinking back. I am cured.

Did the cognitive/motivational therapy work Dr. Zajecka?

Was I ever sick and so I open a can of worms/the contents of the mind? All of the excrement, garbage, refuse (putrifying). Each word carefully chosen so that I can/may accurately represent the contents of the mind. Too much possession. Not dissociation enough of inside from outside. Absolute not temporary merging is dangerous. It leads to a lack of ability to discern truth and deception/deceit. Break apart the nominal from the possessive. Mislead, descriptives, delude (dangerous, eh?) Irony intended. Clarify, elucidate, ingenuate, make true once more, (chute/by-pass,) bounce to future origin.

The father...It's oppressive...always curious...need to know...adjudicate...won't leave me alone...off the back...I already know I can carry you...that's not the point, Christ, not-the-turn, a-joined, dis-connected, torn free, separated, parted (like the line in the hair), disengage, distrust, disavow, dis-case, undo, -ravel, -wind, -case, free, disentangled, screeched, to, a, halt, scratched, dissembling the dots/lines, they don't make sense anymore, you don't exist - Skip! - (and I mean that in the kindest way possible), out. Out-of-rhythm, syncopated, finished, that's it! I've had it! No more! It's a return. A self-addressed sealed envelope. Cul-de-sac. What have you. Not a rejection. A miss. Unhit target. Air.

I tried.

In plain English, I am talking about my right to privacy. It is a miscarriage of justice painted in love with a guise of (true non-lie/deterrence (to use the cold war terminology of the childhood; to date me)/non-pre-emptiveness is missing) respect. I guess everybody lies. That, which is why it is not the lie, I can understand. That, I can forgive. I know.

Therefore I am.

A reversal for Descartes. Animals think. Souls know. Eve, in the garden of Eden, had it right. But I see the logic of pre-knowing. It is important. They say ignorance is bliss. That is not it, exactly. Close, but no cigar. Knowing and not-knowing at the same time, not one before the other. Pre-knowing is the future. To be like someone is to be controlled by that someone which is why ... it may not be the right calling for me. Writing - just had to slip it in there (I distill copied you, Dad) - to be like but not the same (yet another distill copy - according to Homi Bhabha is a resistant, (violent, threatening,) menacing act) and so I blow/unwrap/sequester the self. Benjamin Constant confessions in the 21st century. (Another act of distill copying, followed by pre-knowing this return to the past to pre-create a future (in other words, pre-live-present). Before before before is necessary in order to be pre-original. This is a not-secret not unshared/unknown/un-understood in the world - it's common knowledge. I'm not telling you anything new. Masticate. Digest. Stew. Or more simply, you just have to think about it.

And yet I am not a...

God has the responsibility to make this as easy and painless as possible for strivers-for-pre-cognizance - non-animals (I bring in Stanford here, Akhil Gupta's brilliant) (us) because I know it has the potential to hurt, being me. Toni Morrison's (definition of) love. It's so simple it's brilliant. I think the word they use is elegant when it comes to proof (mathematical, musical): Us - it is help - this pre-knowing-pre-knowing - (or we, in the nominative case, no! yes, English, Professor Akhil Gupta).

Middle.

Before and after at the same time, simultaneously.

There is an overabundance, a surfeit, a nimiety of words. God help! Blessed cursed. Scream... They won't stop.

And yet I must

go to bed

in order (to begin) to feel warm.

It is not a revelation. All that I scriptured (heretic! blasphemous!) above. Because, God dammit, it is sacred text.

Go to Derrida for answers. The centre (I) is the one and only (God). Okay, what I mean is that the self (here I am defending (Zajecka's annoying) the self at not being sick) only recognizes itself in its creation of God (a super-being onto which all desires and aspirations for greatness can be placed) a separate being, which is responsible for all the self's actions. This recognition of self in God is normal. In fact, it is the pre-step to knowing that the self and God are not separate entities. God/the State/--- substitute for the centre, and in this way, the self (I) exists as a doubling (this doubling is the fundamental lie), and the goal of peace is to reunify that separation of self (I) and God/State, so that the self recognizes itself as (I should not have to explain this because it is a reversion to a defense of the self, which is not my responsibility, because (air) you've got the wrong target) of-a-piece, whole. And, quite frankly, I cannot explain you to yourself. Nor I to myself. Because there is only the "self." The reasoning is tautological, which is why it is important to try and escape. A spiral is better than a circle. Even though the annealing of its ends is secure. Perhaps a happy middle ground is both a circle and a spiral so there's something to hold on to while at the same time there's the freedom of letting go.

Without explanation.

Shared knowing.

A (healthy) disregard for etiquette. I burped!

The burp is ever-important. Even though it is not a joke. Even though I don't like it when others (especially men) burp (because I am not in on the joke, in most cases).

Nobody joins me.

Nobody cares.

It is disheartening as a separation (unless, of course, I initiate it, which is not the same thing as somehow knowing).

But this subject is a distraction.

The main point is, I am not sick.

Never was sick.

Had no preconceptions that I was the other. It's ridiculous. Back to defending the self - it is all a figment of the imagination so in reality, there is nothing to worry about, just fears, structured (not by me) pre-conditions for existence. Break free if you can. I have not figured out how.

And so I keep writing. Close but no cigar. Not very cool. We struggle to understand the truth, but the truth constantly evades us, slips through the fingers.

Mesh work.

Stand alone.

Buoyed.

Separate. Icon-not-icon. Non-representation. Real.

A progression from substituted to direct experience. I don't have a Rilke (thank God) (or a Lady Gaga for that matter). For to have a Rilke is to be bound to a precursor when the goal is pre-origination. Everyone has their Rilke. Not unlike Lady Gaga (pop-interpreter of Rilke (and other poets/musicians) for the masses).

Not to be trite.

We are all influenced by the world around us.

Not an excuse.

Nor even an explanation (or is it?).

Just a not-so-innocent observation, which I wish were more naive.

I guess we all project ourselves to greatness.

Scary question: How else will we be buoyed to reach for the stars?

The precariousness of the economy (teetering world-power?) makes us all trepidatious of (shake at) the rustling of (foreign) winds - there is no retreat home for the home has become foreign. An uncommon? Strange, syncopated, unknown ground. We no longer know ourselves, and so we project ourselves into the future and hope for resolution there. The self. It is so hard to be disciplined in order to undiscipline ourselves. Wild. Untamed. The self. Not animal. Soul. In nature. But without copying: like Thoreau. Communion. Love.

Transcendent being still seeking... It is the journey that matters. Love. The journey is the end point, as hard as it is for me to state such a heretical idea. For then we do not unravel. We hold together. True to one another. Pass through the psyche. And arrive on the other side, which is the beginning, untouched. I just wish I weren't on medicine. I do want to believe it helps/is a good thing. I just know I don't believe in it. And that it should not take up as much space in the narrative that it does. Like open heart surgery for the dad. Why? I fight. Don't live in Afghanistan any more (to name it is to call death upon yourself. The self.) (Just a side note to myself: The purpose is less selfish. More pure.) Come home. We miss you. Love you. The empire divides. Dissolves. Maxine Hong Kingston's *Fifth Book of Peace*. Nobody wants to take the blame. Be the scapegoat. Become human. For "us" is souls, not genes. Dissolves (this time only in the most positive sense - didn't know we could turn your meaning on its head, did you? (There is no you. Only us.)) China has the key. Is the way out. (Temporarily). It is not a resolution, merely a path of "non-violence." I don't want to mix and match, but the immigrants (and refugees) have a little insight. Not much. But a little. Enough. To set the world, the universe, on the "right" path. Or some path. At least a path. They know how to walk anyway. Get outta there when the going's tough. Not abandoning. Just departing. Home is too claustrophobic. Honestly. Too much coalescing at once. And so they leave. To make a statement. Or just forge the future. Escape. Not the past, but the forgetting/erasure of the past. Oh well. It still hurts. Just don't name it, pre-name it, and you'll be safe. Happy. Peaceful. Calm. Resolution. It is peace. That is the name. Which you can invoke. Because, to be honest, and sometimes it is necessary to be honest with ourselves, nobody knows. What's in your mind will always be just that, what's in your mind. Safe, sound, peaceful, and secure. I can't help myself. I always give a heads-up just to let people know what's coming. And so I let it be known that I was on the road (must translate here – I am) to becoming a doctor. Unusual - anomolous - as it sounds/is. An M.D. (post-PhD.) Which makes me sad because my mom's a doctor, and I promised myself in youth after I promised myself I would become a doctor, that I would not do what my mom did since it was copying. And I don't copy.

How do I process the processing? It is a meta-question (representation of representation type thing). Writing makes me sick. I feel physically queasy, which makes me think that this processing is not a healthy thing for me to be doing. I am not ready. Future book! The problem is that I do not know if I will ever be ready. The future makes me feel better. Because there is no urgency to arrive at it now. It can wait till tomorrow. I hold on to that thought. There is no pressure. No need to publish it today. In fact, it might be in my best interest not to publish it until after I have got into and even started medical school. There is no telling what they, the school, will do with my information. Labels are labels are labels. No matter how much you try to undo the naming. The explanation can never be enough. It will always fall short. Un-name. The logic falls in on itself. It is just one substitution for another. Metalepsis.

Things fall apart. The centre does not hold. But here the centre holds and remains a series of substitutions. I am sick of substituting. Because at the centre there is nothing. And I keep looking for something. A dissoluble material. Impermanent. But present nonetheless. A key. A touchstone. That would be bliss. Insight. A standard by which to measure the rest. Multiple touchstones. Each to his or her own light. But I am still queasy. For I know this writing is the work of the devil as much as it is the work of God. Therein lies the splitting. Moral crisis. Catechrisis. A dilemma. Truth or no truth. It is possible. For this end, I will fight. A discerning. A splitting of hairs. A King Arthur of modern day. A Guinnevere. Fighting to save the universe. Undo chaos. Impute meaning. Peace. Recognize oneself in the mirror. The many masks we wear are mere illusions. But the illusions are necessary in order to differentiate truth from not-truth. Illusion from reality. Magic from science. Though both need each other for each other's existence. Because the layers protect and ward off danger. They are mutually dependent. But ultimately necessary to separate. The method of separation is through the constant creation and re-creation of the masks. They emphasize and highlight nature. The exaggeration draws attention to key features, so they stick in the memory. Can be recalled and create the ground for recognition. That is the role of Art. As the master of illusion, Merlin points us to the truth. The holy trinity. I cannot claim this knowledge. I can only make feeble attempts. Murky. Earnest. Groping in the dark. For what I do not know. Perhaps Anderson's grotesques reaching out for one another, blind, hoping to one day touch, provide a clue. I do not know. Three-in-one. There is security and fear in the dark. I hope to one day create Art. Not as a magician. Not as a scientist. But as both and neither. On a continuum, gradation, and simultaneously. I, you, "we," to quote myself and Professor Akhil Gupta. It is a joint effort. The more who join the project, the greater it will become, not for its own sake but for the sake of illusion and reality, truth-not-truth. Love-hate. Two sides of the same coin.

Today was a good day. A better day, at least. The writing seems to have calmed me down, and I no longer feel queasy. I know it is not everything that I want to say or how I want to say it, but like Benjamin Constant's *Confessions* and Marcel Proust's *In Search of Lost Time*, the details of my life seem to take on more significance once documented. What bothers me about what I have written above is that I know it is not 100% clear what my meaning is. Basically, I am trying to explain what Art means to me, its role in my recovery process, and what it can hopefully offer the masses, if anyone cares to read this future book.

I have not yet transitioned into a present mode for the book because I do not feel 100% ready to divulge my life story. I want the book to speak to universal truths (if such truths exist) without being self-indulgent. I feel the need to "get behind the ball" not in front of it so that I can keep pushing it, Sisyphus-like, up the hill. Of course, I think I can reach the top. If not, then I will suffer the same fate as Sisyphus. But at least I am trying.

Today, I feel ready to forgive the people who put me in such a horrific situation. I know I'm not stupid and that what happened to me was nobody's fault. From this place, I can forgive. Once I am in medical school and on my way to achieving my goals, I will be at greater peace. I feel closer to this goal and am more calm. Present intrusion into the past: I found out today that I do not have to submit my third quarter grades to medical school, which will be in my favour. What a relief! And once they drop my transcript from Harvard Extension School, when I was sick and could not drop the course I had registered for and subsequently received a 0 since I was hospitalised at that time, I will be happy. I am petitioning for it at the moment, and will be sitting on pins and needles until it (hopefully) goes through. Basically, I feel like I'm going to make it.

Whereas, I did not feel that way these past few days. I am even ready to forgive the medicine. Maybe it is helping. I enjoy eating now, which I did not enjoy doing when I was sick. I knew I had to do it, so I did it, but it was not a source of pleasure. Now I gain pleasure from food. Like I did before I...wow! There it is, before I was sick. So maybe I was sick. Now I feel like I am recovering/have recovered. As long as I have the support of the people around me in this assessment, I am fine. I would like to build a mesh network to support and buoy me up to fame, even though ultimately fame is just a superficial quest. I do have to address my newfound interest in this possibility, embrace it, and move beyond it, because if fame comes along the way so be it, but my primary goal is to live a humble, modest, exciting, and quiet life that involves periods of coming out in public and periods of quiet introspection away from the public eye. Right now I am in the latter phase, but am priming myself for a (or many) future encounters with the public due to my book, my profession, my dreams, hopes and goals. I want to live in a community that supports me. Buoys me up. Validates and values me. I do not want to get lost. As is so easy to do. At the same time, I do not want to live in fear of the unknown, for that is paralyzing. I want to balance insight with action. Premeditation with performance. Reflection and thought with rational (not impulsive or compulsive) decisions. I do not want to do things out of some feeling of compulsion, but rather out of logical desire. A reasoned joy. And I want to execute these activities calmly with the right motivation (to help others) and for the personal satisfaction I get from setting a goal and achieving it. At the moment, my goal is to finish this book. I want it to be 100 pages so that it can be carried anywhere the reader goes and fit into her/his pocket. It is a life-lesson book meant to affix you to your seat because it is so riveting, bring tears to your eyes, it is so moving, change your mind because it is so thought provoking. I want to bring about global change, a revolution of love. And I want to speak to audiences everywhere about these issues as Khaos. Because it is an Art (and a philosophy) that I am transmitting, creating, underscoring, and signifying. Do not accept your suffering for there is always a way out of your situation. Through perseverance, determination, and a recognition of yourself. An identification with yourself. I will be a conduit through which such identification takes place. If you identify with me initially to set you off in the right direction that is fine. Then, it is up to you to riff on that theme, create your own vision, fulfill your own dreams. The masks are important insofar as they serve to ultimately help you recognize the truth, the face beneath the mask. Lady Gaga is a good example of all of these ideas. And she has wrapped them up in packaging that is easily digestible to the masses while still retaining the depth of her Art. That is why I want this book to be no longer than 100 pages because anything more than that will be too long to digest quickly and absorb, like a shot, into your soul. (As long as the medicine helps you). It is time to communicate globally, and we need global figures to help us articulate our sense of isolation, existential dissonance, displacement, and mis-identification. If we no longer recognize ourselves in the mirror, then it is time to make radical adjustments to how we see ourselves. Masks. It is time to see ourselves as integrated, whole selves, not fragmented pieces of shrapnel after a bombing. Touch the mirror and touch yourself. The reflection signifies the real you. You are real. I remember living in Tibet and making a point of always looking at myself in the mirror to remind myself of who I was. It was a survival tactic of sorts. Perhaps not necessary but certainly helpful. I needed to validate that what I saw, though different from the faces I encountered on a daily basis, was a soul behind a face. Eventually, the face did not matter. What mattered were the actions I took (studying, teaching, researching) that reflected my soul. Take apart the artifice and get to the truth. Which is the motivation behind your actions. You must act, as Sartre would insist. But before the act is the intention, and I would argue, like a Tibetan Buddhist might argue, that your motivations count as much or more than the act itself. The two should be commensurate - do not think of a positive aim while killing - that is not justification for the murder. Think of a positive aim while saving someone's life. That is what I mean by commensurate. The rest is history.

## Beauty

How do we define beauty?

An elusive concept intimately tied up with ugly. It is necessary to place each beside the other in order to see the difference.

Exaggeration of features, caricatures, parodies...

all point to the intrinsic beauty of an object. Be it a face, body, work of art, song, video, composition, poem, book...

First there is the original and then there is its parody.

The original is always beautiful. Even if it is the height of ugliness. The uglier it is, the more beautiful. Because that original can always be masked, maligned, exaggerated, accentuated, pulled out of its original shape, distorted...

And it is its return to original form that marks its intrinsic beauty. What we do to objects, that process, is what signifies its meaning as a beautiful object. And so the more copies of that object, improvements upon or malignments of that object, only refer to the original beauty, which is the mark of great Art, and what makes great Art accessible both in its creation by the Artist and comprehension by an observer.

Prisms.

Rainbows.

Light glistening off of lakes.

All are counterposed to the dark.

Shadows.

Clouds.

It is a beautiful symmetry. The contrast between dark and light.

A merging into each other.

With dashes of colour flicked throughout.

Aqua blue, magenta, gold red, orange yellow, peach-fuzz pink. All merge into one and distill out into their fractions. Nothing compares with these reflective times.

Take the time, no matter what you've got going on in your life, to create beauty.

Whether in arranging flowers, opening a window, cracking doors, arraying strawberries.

Each is a sign, symbol, theme, motif. Of beauty yet to come.

Lace a crystal across your neck. Gift it to another. Symbolize your interactions with gifts. Love.

Express your beauty on the outside. Actions speak louder than words.

Write a novel. A sentence. A poem. Signify that beauty.

Identify the crisis. Word it. Manifest it. The struggle.

Struggle reaps beauty. Even in its ugliest forms.

Never doubt yourself. See the struggle manifested, and others will identify with it, see it in their own struggles, their own lives. Connect to the world. Make the private public. Publish! Tell your story.

As many books as there are, there should be that many fold more. An explosion, a profusion of documentation. This époque is now. The time of greatness. Fill it in. Fill up the voids, gaps, spaces. Every blank page is an invitation to speak. Leave your mark and watermark. Know it. Own it to set it free. Let it multiply exponentially into infinity. Simulacra of the soul. This process is a simultaneous veiling and unveiling of beauty. A move toward ugliness to counterpose beauty. Each joined hand-in-hand to complement the other. And, most importantly, to undo the mis-identification. Where you do not recognize the self. And move toward recognition. Create a sentence. A fragment. A run-on. Come out of the dark where you fulminate and into the sun where you shine. Though each stage is necessary. Just as shade prevents you from burning. Horizontal, angled partitions block the burning rays. Light a bulb, a candle to light your way. Shine down a path. And sing! Expose your soul. Play. Be whimsical. And let the colours flick around you. Brief lines of an infinite palette just accentuating your experience, performance, being. Reflecting the pieces of your soul. A beautiful mélange. Separate and coordinated colours. In the end they fade to black, making up the background to your flame. Soul.

And you find in that moment, love. Separate but universal communion, comfort, knowing - not hot nor cold - just together and separate simultaneously - everyone you've ever known and the strangers enter your circle as intimate ami/es. And the circle extends outward into infinity. There are infinite souls. And this is pre-existence. I do not know what comes after death, but I am not scared any more. The universe is one of many existing simultaneously in syncopation with each other. Hold yourself down and exist in beauty/ugliness together. Live at both extremes and everywhere in between. See the beginning, end, and middle together. All of a piece. It is a continuum of a process. A simultaneity. Always on a path toward knowing. Ugliness. A move toward innocence. A revelation of innocence. Pre-knowing. Beauty. Make music! Even if simple, let the tune ring throughout the halls! Melody! Rhythm! Matched by tone/a-tone. Harmony. Empty beats. Remember. Even when the present impinges on a memory, remember. Let the present come, and do not forget where you were before it did so that you may continue recounting your life. The future remains a promise. Tomorrow will come sure as yesterday left and today is. It is hard to fit into the present, and so we constantly attempt to signify it through experiences of the past and promises of the future. Once we become comfortable/fit, the momentum halts, it is difficult to start the macabre dance once again. Escape the pigeon-holing, finger pointing, name calling. And contemplate the process. And the processing of the processing. The escape is in never fitting in. That is, never fitting into the boxes presented to you and always aspiring to create your own place/space without ever settling down into it. It is a universal struggle. This need/attempt to create/make your own space/place. Every man, woman, and child even in those categories, fights against them. Embracing them leads to purposeful exaggerations of them - super-male, hyper-female, uber-kid all pointing to the category itself. Constructed, pre-existence, through preconditions. They (these conditions) might be referred to as "economy," "race," "religion," "gender," "sex," "sexuality," "neighbourhood," "district," "city," "region," "hemisphere," "world," "universe," etc., etc. We are all conditioned by the time/époque/era into which we are born.

Create the world/universe for yourself! Take the scraps and bits of material offered to you by the place/space you were born into and create the world/universe. Not as a part of somebody else's project of world building, but your own! Imagine that world/universe, visualise it, and then construct, engineer, architect, concretize, crystallise, create, make that world. Put the pieces together. Build your vision. Through exaggeration, caricature, parody, excess to accentuate features of that world/universe. Make fun of yourself first in order to make yourself more accessible to the world. In fun lies truth. Or underneath fun lies horror. And in between a liveable place/space. A medium between extremes. Hysteria and horror. Two sides of the same coin. Forged out of the same metal. Tested by the same touchstone. Your heart. Your soul. A truth.

Skip!

Back to the beginning. It is a spiral. A continuation. A reminder of the past, but a progression nonetheless. This spiral defies gravity and moves upward from the ground to the sky - dark, black, clear, foreboding, beautiful. A shade of things to come. In the afterlife. In the pre-life.

## Exposé

What does an exposé reveal? The truth? Interpretations of the truth? Absolute truth? Publicity, attention getting, muck-raking pretensions to the truth? What is the point, purpose of digging through mud to find the kernel of truth? Does that kernel actually exist? Or is the process of obtaining it - smoke and mirrors/illusions/propaganda - the only truth there is in the end. Where the objective is empty, nothing, non-existent. I personally believe in the diaphanous, evanescent, nylon-mesh, dissolving fabric of truth. There-not-there.

And so the exposé reveals this impermanent fabric at the centre that exists and does not exist at the same time. When you want it, it's there. When you don't, it's not. The object is entirely subject dependent. It serves a purpose/function in society just like everything else. Even purposeless objects existing only to act in opposition, as a foil, to the purpose-filled objects. Its purpose is to provide ground when necessary and its absence enables you to deconstruct that ground when necessary. It depends on what you want. Something to hold on to or a disappearing act/emptiness/nothing. Most of us want something but find solace in knowing that perhaps that something is not real. Who wants monsters? If the object of your quest for the holy grail is God, then maybe you want that. Some people don't, and they see monsters in God anyway so it's better for nothing to manifest than this diaphanous, dissolving fabric. I want the option of having the truth exist at times. When I want to validate a feeling. An experience. A struggle. As I do in the Styx series. Malign intentions of my family and the doctors were true as far as I was concerned. They put me in the hospital and restraints in the first place, injecting me with sharp, steel needles all the while. Even if it is the pre-conditions (see Beauty) that led to the series of events leading up to my hospitalisations, I know they were truths that existed. And I want the option of having the truth not exist at other times. A diaphanous web that dissolves in the rain or at the gust of a small wind. Not that my experience was not true. And not that my representation of that experience was not true, but rather that the centre (God/the State/international governing bodies/me) that orchestrates these events, some might call foibles and follies, does not hold/is non-existent.

The writing is the exposé.

Murder is murder is murder. That was the logical conclusion of your acts, Mom and Dad. Crazy! I don't know what to say. It's ineffable. Once again, I am back to a place of speechlessness.

**Death**

This is a contemplation on death.

Death is what renders us speechless (see Exposé). We cannot quantify this event. And because we cannot quantify it, it eludes us. Escapes our comprehension. And if we cannot understand it, we cannot express it.

Surrounding death is fear. The joy we see at funerals masks the tragic nature of the event. We escape into the routine. The life. And the more accoutrements/stuff/things/trappings of life we have, the easier the escape. Food, wine, water, tables, chairs, small talk, even hugs and kisses. Remembering gets us closer to death, but still validates the life lived before death. Why not just talk about the death itself? A passing from this life into the next. An ending point. A beginning point. A middle point. Why a funeral at all? Did I call for this party? It's like celebrating my death day rather than my birthday. And either way, you will have missed the actual moment. Disband with the rituals! There, I said it! I say. Incorporate the body into life, and then it will be okay. Cemeteries are like human landfills. Human garbage dumps. Refuse of the living. The stones mark each body so that there appears to be a logic to the dumping, but it is still dumping. Why ritualise it? Do we all say a prayer on Thursdays when the garbage trucks come by and take our waste to the dump sites? No. So why say a prayer when our bodies are being disposed of?

What I mean to point out here is the disingenuousness of burial in the first place. Cemeteries are body landfills. That is what I am criticizing. There should be some way to preserve the body ad infinitum. Cryogenics may be the answer. Not for the purpose of regenerating those bodies at some point in the future, though that might be nice, but rather for the purpose of continual commemoration of that body. Keep it as close to the living state as possible, not just as a reminder of that life but as a continuation of that life. I guess what I am arguing is a revelation of the fact that humans appear to value life but in death they make a joke of it by throwing bodies away like so much garbage. What is the difference between a mass grave from the holocaust and a cemetery? Not much. Just a few stone markers. And professed logic to the ordering. For me, keep my body. It is/was (for that day when I am no longer alive) a sacred vessel. Incorporate it into your lives. Do not abuse it or make use of it, but treat it as if it were still alive. What is missing in all of those funeral rituals is the dead person him/herself. What kind of party is that? How popular could you have been if you're excluded from your own party? Bring the body forward! Make it the centre of attention! Not just at the wake, but at the party! I guarantee, you will see it smile. No matter how it died, because you remembered it. Keep it together, whole! Of course, it will start to decay. Fall apart. Smell. So freeze it. Inject it with preservatives. But we are already overpopulated! I can hear you argue. There is no space for living-dead bodies. Then why do we make wax museums? What purpose do they serve? They are not ideal because they lump many dead people who may have not had anything to do with each other in one place. If each of those figures were preserved in their house of origin, that would make much more sense. And to pay for a viewing is weird since that person can no longer use the money.

So, back to cemeteries. What to do about this conundrum? Don't bury the dead! How would you like to be put underground? Just like that. So much for respect. Not that I think much of that human artifice. It's just a matter of normalising death. Keep us with you!

We do not want to go! That's what we're afraid of. That physical separation from the world of the living. Just like insane people do not want to be put in madhouses. And sick people do not want to go to the hospital, and old people do not want to be put in nursing homes. They are all movements away from the living and a step closer to death. How mean! And how short-sighted. These movements mark death as different from life when in reality it is not. Mask death through life to reveal death at the last instant (see Book Journal I /Beauty). They are made of the same cloth. Because you could just as easily mask life through death (what I did) to reveal life at the last instant (see Styx). This is Art. Both actions do the same thing. But don't just do it willy-nilly, without thought. Be reflective. Think through your actions. What are you trying to achieve? What point are you trying to make/prove? Have a significant thing to say and then find a way to say it. But of course sometimes our most simple sentiments are the hardest to express and are the ones that require the most masking. Like love. How do we express love?

## Book Journal II

It's like a denouement. A post-climax. The other side of the rainbow. Is there a pot of gold? The Emerald City? No. Just another grassy knoll. Just as beautiful as the original side. Another beginning. An interlude. A middle. A calm. A knowing that whatever happens from this time forward, it is only to wrap up the loose ends of the story. For the story has been told.

But there are more pieces. Perhaps a second climax. After all, being wiped out from telling a story does not mean that that story has been fully told. The other rises and dips are to come. I've told the details of each hospitalisation: 0, 1, 2, and 3. That's four hospitalisations. The last two of which were involuntary. I am still not at peace with these four hospitalisations. They lurk in the background like shadows waiting to pounce. And so I grab them by the tail, and yank them out into the sunlight. They need exposure, just like any gnawing secret. Because each hospitalisation was worse than the one before. More fighting, more restraints, more needles. Even a legal battle. Last hospitalisation. All I remember is the lawyer on the other side of the table yelling, gesticulating, turning red with anger with my sister by his side. I could not imagine why he was so invested in putting me there. In the hospital. Against my will. So angry! I couldn't fathom. It was a huge mystery. What had Erica said to him? The doctor? Either way, it seemed very pointed how he was male and I female. What a jerk. He didn't even know me, and there was no way the doctor knew me. He had just met me. I don't care what kind of expert he was. As respectful, tactful, and civil as I tried to be, I'm sure my disdain for the whole process came through. So there I stayed for two months. The ennui was amazing. Is amazing. We must make meaning out of our lives lest they become vapid reflections of an empty soul. And so I am trying to document these experiences. Without offending, if possible. And the judge looked crazier than anyone, with his robes. I half expected him to don a white, curly wig to top off the effect. What a throw-back to the Middle Ages. The Dark Ages. The whole scene was ridiculous. Me in patient scrubs marking me as different from the rest - as inferior. The judge in black, flowing robes, marking him as different from the rest but as superior. And the rest in business attire attending the hearing - making arguments on one side or on the other. As if the corporate world was a marker of sanity. Whew! What a mess! I'm so glad I got outta there! Even though I had to stay in the hospital for two months, that legal confrontation was the worst part. Just shameful and embarrassing and stupid. It was an unnecessary measure that should never have been taken against me. *One Flew Over the Cuckoo's Nest* is a telling story. Who was insane? The doctors or the patients? Who was really legal? The judge or the defendant? Me, I was legal...innocent! I couldn't believe they were pointing fingers. How rude, uncivil, immoral. I knew I was telling the truth. The rest of them, I couldn't be so sure. It was a farce. Such a play. Such a scene. How out of control! But I recovered. And here I am writing about it. I hope one day to disembowel the statements made against me - word by word. Piece by piece. I have the right to all those documents. It was so ridiculous. I am attempting the disembowelment without the words in front of me through this story/narrative/piecing together of my life over the past ten years. It helps. One word at a time. One sentence at a time. One page at a time. It helps.

The concern is what are the limits of decorum? To what extent can we propagate ourselves without exceeding the limits of acceptability?  Of course, the point is to push those limits.  Wake people up.  Rouse them from their slumber.  Shake up the world a little bit so as to let the pieces settle back into new and provocative places. So they question the original edifice in the first place.  I want to wake people up.  Motivate them to love.  Inspire greatness.  That is what this book is.  My method is exposé.  "Confessions" according to Benjamin Constant.  A form of self-revelation.  A recollection of time past/wasted time according to Marcel Proust.  A signifying of a life.  Because all has not gone as planned.  I followed the yellow brick road, and it turned black as the asphalt passing beneath the ambulance. No Emerald City.  No munchkins.  No Wizard of Oz to return me home.  Not even a pair of ruby slippers.  Only bare feet, brown brick facades and clinical white interiors.  Imprisonment by the Wicked Witch of the West.  And her henchmen, not monkeys, but white coated orderlies commanded to restrain me and poke me with needles.  The nightmare continues.  These memories haunt me but do not comprise me.  I am above them.  Separate from them.  I want them to crystallize out of me so that I may identify and name them.  Not necessarily destroy them, but display them as separate from me.  As coming from a mixture not of my making but of my hand.  A pollutant.  A contamination.  An impurity.  Some of them may look beautiful.  Others offensive to the senses.  Either way, it is the naming that is important.  Hospitalisation 0, 1, 2, 3, etc.  Though they keep crystallizing out even when the finished product should have long precipitated. More fragments of glass.  There is likely an endless supply of super-saturated solution, which is why the process is not finished.  So endpoints are not easy to come by.

# Styx

It's like leaky windows to an otherwise sealed house. Impenetrable to storms but somewhere there's a break. The past keeps intruding on the present. The present interrupting the narrative of the past. Nothing streams. Is linear. All is broken. Segmented. Fragmented. And the drips dripping inward ruin the carpet, the walls, the paint, the furniture, the foundation of the house. And you need that house for protection. But maybe it is that house that keeps you locked in. A prison. A madhouse. So the memories serve a purpose. You're just not sure you're ready for them. In fact, you're sure you're not ready for them. They flood. Cover you. Overwhelm you. Drown you. Like in my nightmares. The last thing you want, however, is for somebody else to codify your experiences for you (or against you). So write them, mark them, name and signify them. If for no other reason than to clarify yourself to yourself and the world. And if the world receives only murky meanings, then at least you made the effort. Took the risk to expose yourself and all those secrets. Thoughts. Feelings. Experiences. Traumas. Horrors. Because they build in the system until one day, the dam breaks. And there is seepage, spillage, a tidal wave, tsunami. Wreaking havoc on you and the people around you. So it is better to modulate the water's release. You control it. Nobody else. Some people can see what you've written/said/expressed. And when you're ready to deliver the tidal wave, the world will be waiting with open arms to receive your flood. Because there are enough people in the world to absorb your meaning. To signify with you. It is just a matter of reaching those souls, isolated or not, that feel something is awry, or dead wrong, with the system. Not just a misalignment of justice. A malignment of justice. Who is right and who is wrong? I am with Gandhi and Martin Luther King, Jr. No violence for me. Resist. Resist. Resist. Justice will raise its shining head one day and light the path for all.

Toward love. Toward peace. Toward equality. Do not treat me as a criminal. As an insane person. As incapacitated or beyond good judgement. Ever. Not then. Not now. Or in the future. Do not give me respect, that attribute of civility, give me soul. Not humanity. Soul. Feeling. Connection. Understanding. Empathy. Like you know what I'm talking about. Like you've been there. Seen that. Know. Filter your words so that they do not harm. Pick and choose your adjectives. Create peace. Build a monument to love. Sticks and stones...

But do not lie. Deceive. Mislead.

Disingenuity destroys meaning.

Leave yourself open to love.

Crush your inhibitions. Leave your anxiety at the door. Angst-be-gone...worry no more. Even the score. Do not give up hope. Nothing to smash you...beyond this book's scope. Love will prevail. Happiness in the end. Through this art, your soul will sail. Believe in yourself and your words will come through. Meaning and all, I promise you. I know from experience, that you can succeed, if you envision the end that satisfies your need to expose your soul and reveal its depths. Shadows and darkness fall - small steps. Gradations and shades cover and protect while you decide what to eject. In time, all will tell, the story in toto unfolds. Say what you must to reveal the mold. Stand as creator, decide your fate. Take brave steps to abolish hate. In your story and yours alone, the truth stands out and sinners atone.

I make this promise because I know that beyond catharsis is a conquered foe. Death, hate, and animosity. Our lives continue into infinity. Black ink, indelible words link to reveal the truth, the undying proof of my love for you, dear reader. Because I must pass the word, like a flame into infinity, beyond the absurd. Say what you must to express your heart. Be true to yourself, and you'll find your start, the beginning of the narrative, the sentiment of middle, and finally an end. Deception fails, disguise and lie, so try to sail, try not to hide. A mask or veil serves its purpose of pointing to the truth beneath the veneer, but in the end, the soul must come clear. So we know nothing was there. Everything and nothing combine to grow the mind and make clear that nobody loses and winners disappear.

There are myriad diamonds lighting the sky, illuminating the darkness, and together we fly. Not all as one or fragmented wholes, but recombinatory pieces that gradually unfold. Separate. Together. We are all of a piece. Love one another, create your niche. A place in the world, the universe, where we do not rock or fall prey to the curse of dissonant lives out of sync with the times. We are present, but not fixed. Here, but not whisked into a never-land of pigeon-holes so bland they determine our fates without will power to counter infinite hates. Liberate yourself, construct your future, live your dream, do not get caught in other's ideations, which fulfill their quest and drown your own. Find a dream and make it happen. Visualise the endpoint and live it. Singing your song. Reciting your poetry. Reading your book. Citing it entirely from memory - it's that ingrained in your soul/skin/being. Keep questing. But not for empty endpoints. Make your dreams concrete so others see. You will not be invisible any more. While protecting your anonymity. Dream.

**Freedom**

What is freedom?  We seek self-definition in order not to mis-identify with ourselves - a cause of existential dissonance and disjuncture.  The world offers up a mirror, and if what we see in its reflection is not us, then there is dissonance.  Fear is the opposite of freedom, but bravery is not its synonym since many a brave act might also be considered mindless and even stupid. Happiness and freedom can go hand-in-hand but are by no means definitive partners.  Getting over past relationships is a source of happiness.  Recovering from trauma is a source of happiness.  Un-ghosting horrors is a source of happiness.  These happinesses can all lead to a sense of freedom.  But what is real freedom?  The ability to write without self-censorship?  Fame?  Wealth? Knowledge?  Power?

For example, there is so much balled/walled up inside of me that I know I am not yet free.  There are demons that haunt me and intrude into my everyday existence.  It all began the day before my MCAT, April 30th, 2010. Suddenly, I had the urge to document my hospitalisations.  Embark on a project entirely different from my medical school pursuits.  One that I hoped would set me free.  And there's the rub.  I am not ready, nor do I wish, to give up on my medical school aspirations.  At the same time, the urge to write overtakes me every day, and I must document my existence as if my life depended on it.  And perhaps it does, in some unconscious way.  I see others, famous people, celebrities, making meaning out of their lives, calling it Art, documenting, somehow, their experiences. I would like to do the same without copying them.  For there is a shallowness to celebrity, which would render my life even more meaningless than it is now - not that I think I lead a meaningless existence; it's just that I know

I could be leading a much more meaningful existence if I could touch people with my Art. Writing, composing, music (one day). Each leads to the next and all are of a piece. I am no better and no worse than anyone else, but I do have a lot to say. I want people to know the full me so that they can understand me, inquire about me, ask questions. What could be more flattering than to be questioned about your life? Not interrogated, mind you; nor criticized, but questioned because some idea or other that you documented resonated with your questioner. There is freedom in dialogue. Conversation. Open discussion. Language. Creating language.

What makes us normal? Is there any connection with normality and freedom? There is always the cover of normality. But what lies beneath? Who defines what is normal? What are the parameters? I know I dislike the disease manual produced for doctors in order to come up with diagnoses for their patients. It seems that our definition of what is normal restricts our freedom rather than guaranteeing it.

I guess when I talk of freedom, I speak of it in the artistic sense of self-expression/re-presenting experience. Or rather providing direct experience through Art. Evoking a feeling, sense, time, place - provoking an emotion, reaction, action. These are all goals of my Art. To achieve this end would be to achieve a dream and in that sense arrive at a form of freedom. I realise, as I get older, that writing is the first step. Creating an audience for your work is the next necessary and vital step to thriving as an Artist. I want that give and take between me and my fans. And yes, I am willing to go so far as to say, I aim for a worldwide, expansive, massive fan base. Why? The more people who can relate to my Art, the more inspired I am to produce it. Nobody wants to talk in a vacuum. And so I am actively seeking a literary agent. A publisher. My goal is to get my Art out to the masses. Why am I including this train of thought in my book? Why in a section on freedom? Because to create a vision and have it recognized let alone received by the world is the goal of any Artist. I will produce regardless, but I thirst for that dialogue. The response to my work. Letters, e-mails, requests, notes...anything, everything. Touch the world.

I am writing from a very scary place. The risk I take is great because I could be exposed at any point before safety nets have been put in place - like anonymity in a pen name, copyrights, etc. I imagine I will write under a pen name, an Art name, for as long as it is necessary to build up a fan base. I am happy to have people know my real name, but when it comes to my Art refer to me by my Art name. At the moment, this name is Khaos in reference to the Greek primordial deity of the nothingness that preceded existence. The name is serious. Though I realise it could come off as trite, fake, pretentious, forced, or simply unnecessary. But the subject matter with which I deal is so devastating and potentially harmful to my reputation due to the stigma associated with it, that I have chosen to maintain anonymity for the time being. It may be a Richard Bachman to a Stephen King, who knows. Maybe one day I will not need the pseudonym. Today, I need it. For me, authenticity is in the Art. Revelation can come later, when the world is ready for it. Right now the world is too young to handle subject matter like psychosis. It is automatically associated with crime and criminality. When I first heard the term used to describe me, I almost died. What an insult! A crime! I, a psychotic!? What a ridiculous claim! The more I learn about the disease, the more I am sure I am right to revolt against the naming. And this brings us back to the subject of freedom, which I have never left. While naming can be a creative act, it can also be a destructive act - moreover, an imprisoning act. So to take the name and turn it on its head or use it cleverly or infuse it with revolutionary and new meaning has been one way to fight the name-calling. See "queer," "n-----," etc. Here, I mean to tell the people who are calling out the names, namely doctors, to stop doing so. The categories are limiting, paralyzing, offensive, misplaced. Sticks and stones... The naming does do harm. I am writing it to demonstrate that the invocation of psychotic actuates restraints, medicine, needles, ostracising, and institutionalisation. In short, criminalisation. The system is not broken. The system is too efficient. And it is this efficiency, which leads to broken bodies and broken minds of those subject to its call.

And the medicine changes the shape of your brain so that you cannot exist, think, nor act without it. It IS a kind of dependency. I learned this the hard way when, after being on medicine for four years, I tried to take myself off of it under the supervision of two psychiatrists and ended up not being able to think, write, read, or process as I had before being put on the medicine. I hold and firmly believe that I was incapacitated after being taken off of the medicine not because the medicine was fixing something that had gone wrong in my brain but because the medicine itself had induced a change in my brain such that my brain required the artificial substance in order to function normally. After all, when I was taken off of the medicine the first time after 9 months of being on it, I lived for three years without any problems. Out of the country, no less. Not under the supervision of any psychiatrist. The medicine had not altered the shape of my brain enough to induce dependency. Why did I go back on the medicine if I was doing fine? Because upon returning to the U.S., my mother insisted I was sick, referred me to Dr. Zajecka, who wanted the business, and the two of them put me back on the medicine - this time coupled with anti-depressants. I eventually managed to get off of the anti-depressants because I did not believe in them, and am still off anti-depressants. But when I tried to get off the other medicine, my brain broke down. I could not process properly, write, read, etc. I still do not believe I am sick. I now believe I am stuck on medicine (involuntarily) for the rest of my life. It is a prison not of my own making. I challenged the order of things, and people, namely men, got threatened. The women who intervened to make sure I went back on the medicine, namely my mother, did so because it was the least worse thing that she could do to ensure I was not incarcerated or worse. I wholly believe she was trying to protect me, just as women in East Africa want to protect their daughter's sexuality to ensure a good marriage by giving them a clitoridectomy. Well, mine was a clitoridectomy of the brain. Which is worse? They are definitely comparable. I must have threatened the status quo somehow. So I give you the pretty form of my experience through Art. It could land me in jail or worse, I suppose. Except that there's that pesky First Amendment. Not that I believe in the concept of "rights" since it is based on the idea of the Enlightenment individual - the same unit of society that justified slavery. However, I do believe it is possible to re-infuse words with new meaning, and I would like to associate the protection of rights with freedom.

Out of control is not freedom. Just like total control is not freedom. The middle, in between, is freedom. Measured words but not censored. Outlandish statements but not offensive. Somewhere between decorum and rude. Skating between these extremes. The importance of being free. Not in a fantasy world, although sometimes our fantasies are a conduit to freedom, but rather in the real world. Wearing what you want when you want. Asking for acceptance and receiving it. Getting accepted regardless. Not without rules but based on the inherent integrity of your character. Finding what you want even when you receive the opposite. An ice-cream sundae out of an orange. A palace out of a hovel. A dream out of a nightmare. It is all in the working of the stitches. The imagination is freedom. Or rather actualising the imagination. Manifesting/concretising dreams. Crystallising a vision. I see the future - performing quietly, loudly, in whispers and screams in front of millions, no, billions. The world waiting with baited breath for the mere utterance of a word from my lips. And then, absolute silence. Total quiet. A moment of communion - with each other, with the universe. I will be my Art. Not just perform it. Be it. Live it, breathe it, be it. Articulations of me. And then, I will have silences of my own. In my own space. On my own time. With my own soul. Dream.

**Book Songs**

Song I:  The Door

I. I see this window.

I see this door.

The world is open before me.

I know how to soar.

Crack the window.

Crack the door.

Leave it ajar.

For the wind to give me more.

Lift my wings.

Carry me into the night.

Before day breaks.

And I am lost  to flight.

Chorus: Sing. Sing. Sing.

There is more to the world than meets the eye.

Dance. Dance. Dance.

Move your body until you die.

(Repeat Chorus)

II. It  is a chorus of love.

A meaning of truth.

# Styx

A quest for soul.

A moment of proof.

You see me sitting there.

You wait.  You pass me by.

Where is the soul?

When all you had to do was try.

Reach out.

Touch your neighbour.

Make new friends.

Take a chance.  Open the door.

Chorus: Sing. Sing. Sing.

There is more to the world than meets the eye.

Dance. Dance. Dance.

Move your body until you die.

(Repeat Chorus)

III.  The time is near.

I now must close.

Before I go.

My eye sees what it knows.

Your eyes.

Your face.

Your lips.

Your taste.

It is you that sets me free.

Chorus: Sing. Sing. Sing.

There is more to the world than meets the eye.

Dance. Dance. Dance.

Move your body until you die.

(Repeat Chorus)

Song II:  Fall

I.  Knowing only makes it hurt more.

That you lied in order to score.

You lost me on the way out.

And kept your secret,  soft and loud.

What's in it for me...in the lies you told?

Now, I'm only getting old.

Passing time with you by my side.

Is just a dream I try to hide.

Do I regret?

Do I forget?

I don't lose the song.

You lost what made us one.

# Styx

So keep on crying when you hear my name.

You always knew love would bring me fame.

And so I harp on what I know.

Love, love, love...I told you so.

Chorus: Sing! Sing! Sing!

Dance! Dance! Dance!

You know this is your last chance!

Sing! Sing! Sing!

Dance! Dance! Dance!

To find my heart with love's romance.

Repeat chorus.

II.  Think again.  Think twice and hard.

Why did you leave when so on guard?

Defenses high, fighting stance.

Didn't you think we had a chance?

It happened when you stopped to fall.

It was in your eyes.  You had no wall.

You fell for her.  I could see not me.

But beneath it all, I was free.

Do I lie?

Do I try?

You lost what made us free.

I recovered.  I got me.

Take this cue.  Your time is up.

I've had enough.  You know what's up.

In your escape, I made mine too.

You from me, and me from you.

Chorus: Sing! Sing! Sing!

Dance! Dance! Dance!

You know this is your last chance!

Sing! Sing! Sing!

Dance! Dance! Dance!

To find my heart with love's romance.

Repeat chorus.

In the end, it's for the best.

I do not pine for what is less.

Take me now.  Take me forever.

I am yours.  Torn, now, together.

Reality bites, but I'm no fool.

Take her too, and you're just a tool.

In the end, it's just a game.

So watch your heart, just the same.

# Styx

I fell for you once before.

This time I think you know the score.

The game's been played.

Time's running out.

She or I?  I have no doubt.

Time is up. I'll count to three.

Without you, we two are free!

Chorus: Sing! Sing! Sing!

Dance! Dance! Dance!

You know this is your last chance!

Sing! Sing! Sing!

Dance! Dance! Dance!

To find my heart with love's romance.

Repeat chorus.

Song III: Beat

Nobody knew us.  We thought we were free.

Until the time came when you beat me.

And I realized that was not love.

It must be you were sent from above.

To teach me how to love myself.

And escape your fist and begin to delve

Into my soul to know the truth.

Nobody saw.  There was no proof.

Until one day.  The day I died.

I saw them take you by the side.

And hook your arms into cold chains.

Where you would die until I came

Back from the dead to teach this song.

There's no beating - you know you're wrong.

So listen to my ghost sing to your soul.

God can save you if you let go

Of the hate and fear and misery.

Just let me go.  Let me be me.

Chorus:  There's still joy!  There's still glee!

Come back from the dead.   Where you'll be free.

There's still joy!  There's still glee!

There's no more pain beyond you and me.

Repeat Chorus.

Even in death you hold your grip.

So I must fight until you're whipped

And everybody else can see

That you are just as good as me.

# Styx

Dead.

My friend.

Dead.

It started with desire and led to death.

Two souls entwined till their last breath.

Jean-Paul Sartre knew his stuff.

He would have said, "Enough is enough!"

And given us a clue to the end of it.

In life and death, there is No Exit.

We suffer with each other.  We suffer without.

You beat me.  I haunt you out.

My ghost delves within your soul

To teach you lessons you couldn't know.

While alive, I suffered blows.

But now, while dead, I aid your foes.

Whisper your reason to me

For treating me like I was three.

Chorus:  There's still joy!  There's still glee!

Come back from the dead.   Where you'll be free.

There's still joy!  There's still glee!

There's no more pain beyond you and me.

Repeat Chorus.

I'll proclaim an undying love.

The key will fit, like hand-in-glove.

Do I lie?

Do I cry?

What point is there from beyond the grave?

Follow your heart. It's a choice God gave.

Risk the truth. It will set you free.

Admit your past. And I will leave.

We'll obliterate the cycle of death.

And only then on your dying breath.

Once you admit you beat me down

and ask forgiveness while I'm around.

There'll be ten million reasons to live.

Though you might be dead, I'll still forgive.

So raise yourself up. Your time has come.

It's a celebration. The world is numb.

To death and destruction and misery.

And in the end, you'll find me.

Chorus: There's still joy! There's still glee!

Come back from the dead. Where you'll be free.

There's still joy!  There's still glee!

There's no more pain beyond you and me.

Repeat Chorus.


Song IV: Pray

Silver, gold, sunshine falling down.

I see your face in my reflection.

Off the water, in the sea, all over this town.

Between you and me, there is no separation.

This song lifts us up to where we belong.

Higher than skies, taller than stars.

Before time flies, before we are gone.

Reach for the moon, go beyond Mars.

Chorus: Our union, our communion.

There is only one way.

Our union, our communion.

The light shines as we pray.

Repeat chorus.

You'll find me there waiting for you.

Holding your picture in my mirror.

Where there was one, now there's two.

The Milky Way knows what's in store.

Follow the trail of diamonds left behind.

On sunny shores in Mediterranean seas

You'll see what's yours and what is mine

As long as you follow the shining trees.

Chorus: Our union, our communion.

There is only one way.

Our union, our communion.

The light shines as we pray.

Repeat chorus.

Milky light pours down on me,

Now I know that we are free,

Not a boy or a girl, a he or a she,

Just a song about a swinging tree.

Where we fit in this wide, wide world.

A universe opening up beyond the edge.

Understanding all the broken words.

Finding the will to make a pledge.

Chorus: Our union, our communion.

There is only one way.

Our union, our communion.

## Styx

The light shines as we pray.

Repeat chorus.

www.ingramcontent.com/pod-product-compliance
Lightning Source LLC
Chambersburg PA
CBHW021158010426
R18062100001B/R180621PG41931CBX00015B/25